Economic Reforms,
Regionalism, and Exports:
Comparing China and India

Policy Studies 60

Economic Reforms, Regionalism, and Exports:
Comparing China and India

Ganeshan Wignaraja

*Economic Reforms, Regionalism, and Exports:
Comparing China and India*
Ganeshan Wignaraja

ISSN 1547-1349 (print) and 1547-1330 (electronic)
ISBN 978-1-932728-94-1 (print) and 978-1-932728-95-8 (electronic)

Hard copies of all titles, and free electronic copies of most titles, are available from:

East-West Center
1601 East-West Road
Honolulu, Hawai'i 96848-1601
Tel: 808.944.7111
EWCInfo@EastWestCenter.org
EastWestCenter.org/policystudies

In Asia, hard copies of all titles, and electronic copies of select Southeast Asia titles, co-published in Singapore, are available from:

Institute of Southeast Asian Studies
30 Heng Mui Keng Terrace
Pasir Panjang Road, Singapore 119614
publish@iseas.edu.sg
bookshop.iseas.edu.sg

Contents

List of Acronyms

ADB	Asian Development Bank
APTA	Asia-Pacific Trade Agreement
ASEAN	Association of Southeast Asian Nations
BIS	Bank for International Settlements
BRIC	Brazil, Russia, India, and China
CECA	Comprehensive Economic Cooperation Agreement
CEPA	Comprehensive Economic Partnership Agreement
ECFA	Economic Cooperation Framework Agreement
EFTA	European Free Trade Association
EPZ	export processing zone
EU	European Union
FDI	foreign direct investment
FTA	free trade agreement
FICCI	Federation of Indian Chambers of Commerce and Industry
G-20	Group of Twenty Finance Ministers and Central Bank Governors
GATS	General Agreement on Trade in Services
GATT	General Agreement on Tariffs and Trade

GDP	gross domestic product
HS	Harmonized Commodity Description and Coding System
ICT	information and communications technology
IT	information technology
ITA	Information Technology Agreement
IMF	International Monetary Fund
LDC	least developed country
MFN	most-favored nation
MNC	multinational corporations
NTM	nontariff measures
OECD	Organisation for Economic Co-operation and Development
PPP	purchasing power parity
R&D	research and development
RCA	revealed comparative advantage
REER	real effective exchange rate
SAFTA	South Asia Free Trade Area
SEZ	special economic zone
SME	small- and medium-sized enterprise
SPS	Agreement on the Application of Sanitary and Phytosanitary Measures
TBT	Agreement on Technical Barriers to Trade
TPP	Transpacific Strategic Economic Partnership Agreement
TVE	township and village enterprises
UN Comtrade	United Nations Commodity Trade Statistics Database
WITS	World Integrated Trade Solution
WTO	World Trade Organization

Executive Summary

Against the backdrop of recovery from the global financial crisis, this paper attempts to reappraise the links between economic reforms and exports in China and India, the "giants." Four questions are analyzed: (1) Have China's exports outpaced India's since the reforms? (2) What roles have initial conditions, as well as liberalization of trade and investment regimes, played in the giants' export records? (3) Is the giants' recent emphasis on free trade agreements (FTAs) detrimental to exports? (4) What are the emerging policy challenges in the post–global financial crisis era?

Beginning in the 1950s, the giants followed inward-oriented, state-controlled economic strategies. Various economic distortions, including high import protection and state-directed resource allocation, held back the private sector and exports. In a radical break with past economic policies, China and India adopted market-oriented economic reforms in the late 1970s to boost exports and the private sector. More recently, they have pursued FTA-led regionalism alongside multilateralism. Few foresaw the future impact the giants would collectively have on world trade patterns, or the magnitude of adjustment required in rest of the world.

There is little doubt that the trade performance of China and India has been impressive by the standards of either developing countries or developed countries. Within a relatively short time span of about a generation, the two countries have emerged as major players in world trade, as well as notable outward investors. Following early entry into low-technology products, the giants have steadily upgraded into medium- and high-technology products, as well as skill-intensive services. While the two are often compared, China has roared ahead in world trade of manufactures and is on the verge of challenging the United States as the world's largest exporter. India's export expansion has been primarily driven by services, and it is attempting to play catch-up in a range of manufactured exports.

The outcome of economic reforms on trade performance was shaped by initial conditions. These include China's proximity to Japan, which facilitated inward investment and a large, dynamic domestic market. Township and village enterprises (TVEs) also seem to have led labor-intensive rural industrialization in China in the 1980s and early 1990s. Both India and China had access to ample supplies of low-cost, productive manpower. India's relative success in information technology and business process outsourcing seems linked to exposure to English, world-class information technology (IT) professionals and engineers, and close links with an IT-oriented diaspora.

Reforms of trade and investment, in particular, have played a significant role in the trade performance of China and India. China, of course, was swifter and introduced an open door policy toward export-oriented foreign direct investment (FDI) in the late 1970s, alongside controlled liberalization of imports. Further liberalization occurred in China during the process of World Trade Organization (WTO) accession. India introduced some reforms in the late 1970s, but the major reforms came after 1991. The difference in trade performance between China and India, however, is not simply a matter of the timing of changes in trade and investment policies. Closer examination suggests China adopted a more comprehensive and pro-active approach to trade and industrial policy than did India. In its efforts to attract export-oriented FDI, it actively facilitated technological upgrading of FDI and exports, reduced import tariffs and the dispersion of tariffs in a more systematic manner, managed a more predictable and transparent real effective exchange rate (REER), and provided for more comprehensive liberalization in goods and services provisions in its FTAs with Asian developing economies.

India's 1991 economic reforms marked the end of the license raj and heralded the start of a more conducive investment climate for the private sector. In recent years, India has attempted to put in place appropriate trade and investment policies, particularly for attracting export-oriented FDI and liberalizing tariffs. It is also attempting to conduct ambitious FTA negotiations with developed countries that could provide market access and FDI inflows, among other benefits.

Therefore, one might reasonably expect the gap in trade and investment performance between the giants to narrow over time, but China's dominance in manufactures is expected to continue for at least the next decade. Some popular accounts predict that India's growth may overtake China's by 2013. Several factors are said to lie in India's favor, including a relatively young and growing workforce, a base of world-class companies led by English-speaking bosses, and democratic institutions. Weighed against this is a much larger export base in China; much higher levels of investment in research and development (R&D), workforce skills, and infrastructure; and better policy coordination and implementation.

Both China and India face a new and more uncertain world economic environment in the post–global financial crisis era. The global financial crisis marked the end of a period of respectable world growth and expanding employment in major industrial economies. The likely scenario for the medium term seems to be slow growth and high unemployment in large swaths of the developed world. Rebounds in China and India provided critical support for the world economy. Meanwhile, China and India have seen a resurgence of growth since the global financial crisis, and they have contributed to world growth during and after the crisis. However, it is unclear how much the giants can extend this role without a stronger recovery in the developed world.

Myriad policy challenges are likely to impinge on the pace of China's and India's trade-led growth in the new macroeconomic era. Challenges include: entering production networks, promoting industrial technology development, investing in infrastructure, reducing red tape, increasing FTA use by businesses, managing exchange rates, mitigating the risk of protectionism, and reducing poverty. The effect of this new economic era on trade performance in the giants will depend crucially on how each copes with these challenges.

Economic history suggests that the center of economic gravity will continue to shift toward Asia, with the giants playing a growing role in the region's prosperity. China and India seem set to increase their dominance of world trade in the next decade; adapting trade and investment policies, along with other measures, will play a notable role in that success. The twenty-first century seems to have all the markings of an Asian century.

Economic Reforms, Regionalism, and Exports:
Comparing China and India

1. Introduction

This paper examines the influence of economic reforms on exports in the Asian giant economies of China and India since the late-1970s. Economic reforms are defined here as the opening up of the economy to foreign trade and investment, the removal of restrictions on private sector activities, and the introduction of markets in a centrally planned economy. A distinction is sometimes made between reforms at the border and reforms behind the border. The former, which is this paper's focus, are reforms to liberalize trade and investment flows through a vibrant private sector. These were at the core of economic reform programs in China since 1978, and in India since 1991. The latter reforms—such as competition policy to mitigate the abuse of monopoly power and trade facilitation to simplify customs procedures—were also relevant to the giants, but were excluded here because of lack of data.

The steep rise of China and India in world trade has attracted considerable recent attention, understandably so. The giants have rapidly moved from agricultural backwaters to huge global exporters within a few decades. Already they collectively make about 13 percent of world exports, which is increasingly comprised of technologically sophisticated manufactures and services. And the giants' exports have rebounded faster than many others following the global financial crisis. Rapid trade-led growth has lifted hundreds of millions out of poverty in both economies. The giants' record in world trade is noteworthy in two respects. First, their influence on world trade beginning in the late-1970s was largely unforeseen. Informed analysts note that China's performance "already has been the largest growth surprise ever experienced by the world economy" (Winters and Yusuf 2007, 1) and project the two giants to be among the world's largest trading economies within a couple of decades (Winters and Yusuf 2007; Maddison 2007). Second, their trade performance is admirable by any standards, whether it is compared to newly industrializing economies in Asia or large, developed countries in the West (Amsden 2001; Maddison 2007; Gerhaeusser, Iwasaki, and Tulasidhar 2010). Recent international events (e.g., the global financial crisis, the slow recovery in the United States, and the disasters in Japan) are likely to hasten the rise of China and India in world trade. This has implications for both the giants and the rest of the world.

The global financial crisis and slow US recovery may hasten China's and India's rise in world trade

A popular, conventional picture of the giants' role in world trade underscores the notion that their remarkable trade performance and their adoption of market-oriented economic reforms are causally related (see, for instance, Holscher, Marelli, and Signorelli 2010). This account suggests the giants pursued inward-oriented, centrally planned development strategies that caused multiple distortions and hampered exports and private sector activity. The adoption of economic reforms improved resource allocation and prompted a shift to a more market-oriented economy. The entry of export-oriented, foreign direct investment (FDI) through fiscal incentives facilitated the move from import substitution to the production of manufactures for export. Little differentiation is made between either the trade performance or the timing of economic reforms of the giants.

Yet empirical evidence on the simple causal link between trade performance and economic reforms is mixed. Four lines of recent applied research can be distinguished. One line of research differentiates between the export record and the reforms of China and India. India is credited with turning the corner since the adoption of reforms, but its export performance is believed to be in a different league from China's, which is linked to the timing of liberalization (Lardy 2003; Panagariya 2006 and 2007; Kowalski 2010). A second line of research recognizes the role of opening up markets, but suggests that active industrial policies in China played a complementary role in nurturing domestic capabilities in consumer electronics and other advanced areas that may not have developed in their absence (e.g., Amsden 2001; Rodrick 2006). Implicit in this line of thinking is that the absence of industrial policies since 1991 may, in part, explain why India lags behind China in advanced manufactured exports. A third line of research suggests that the giants have been engaged in global trade liberalization, as well as preferential trade liberalization, to foster regional integration. It expresses concerns that the giants' recent pursuit of free trade agreements (FTAs) may be detrimental to exporting due to the shallow coverage of agreements and an Asian "noodle bowl" of overlapping FTAs (Baldwin 2008; Suominen 2009). A fourth line of research has begun investigating the effects of new policy challenges facing the rising giants in the post–global financial crisis world. These include the risk of protectionism, exchange rate management, business use of FTAs, and poverty reduction (Asian Development Bank 2011a; Bardhan 2010; Cline 2010; Feenstra and Wei 2010; Kawai and Wignaraja 2011; Sen 2011).

Accordingly, China's and India's experiences with exports and economic reforms may not fit this popular, conventional picture. The four lines of research outlined above suggest that the mix of trade and investment policies is both more complex and rapidly evolving. This paper undertakes a comparative economic analysis of the link between economic reforms and export performance in China and India, with a view to indicating similarities and differences. While a plethora of insightful studies exist on economic reforms and trade patterns in either China or India, comparative economic analysis of the giants' experiences is a relatively new area of recent economic research.[1] Furthermore, most studies were written before the global financial crisis. Rapidly evolving international events highlight the imperative for research on trade and investment implications of the giants' rise in the post–global financial crisis world. This paper uses new information and research to analyze the past record. It also tries to offer pragmatic solutions to evolving policy challenges.

The comparative analysis in the paper is framed around four interesting questions concerning economic reforms and exports in the giants:

1. Have China's exports outpaced India's since the reforms?

2. What roles have initial conditions, as well as liberalization of trade and investment regimes, played in the giants' export records?

3. Is the giants' recent emphasis on FTAs detrimental to exports?

4. What are the emerging policy challenges in the post–global financial crisis era?

Section 2 examines the first question about whether China's exports have outpaced India's by tracing the evolution of trade flows in the giants at the aggregate and sectoral levels. It examines data on trade growth and world market shares, the composition of manufactured exports using a technology-based classification, services export growth and composition, and revealed comparative advantage at the sector level.

Sections 3 and 4 deal with the second question, which is the central issue of the paper. Section 3 briefly discusses the role played by key initial conditions (e.g., geography, market size, skill base, and institutions) in shaping the giants' overall export record. Section 4 explores the link between trade and investment reforms and trade flows. For both India and China, it provides an assessment of trade and investment reforms and export outcomes, as well as some comparisons between the giants' reform strategies. To set the stage, some stylized facts on the pre-reform trade and investment regimes highlight economic distortions that arose from inward-oriented strategies in China and India. Subsequently, an analysis is made of the extent of liberalization of trade and investment regimes that occurred during the outward-oriented period. Using standard indicators of trade and investment liberalization—such as deregulation of FDI rules and growth in FDI inflows and outflows, reform of import control instruments and trends in import tariffs, and exchange rate reforms and evolution of the real effective exchange rate—an evaluation is made of the reforms and export outcomes.

Section 5 examines the third question of whether recent moves towards FTAs have been detrimental to exporting. It evaluates FTA quality in terms of some simple criteria and provides evidence on the use of FTAs at the firm level. Section 6 explores the fourth question about emerging policy challenges in the post–global financial crisis era and solutions. It discusses several issues, including entering production networks, promoting industrial technology development, increasing FTA use by business, investing in infrastructure and reducing red tape, managing exchange rates, dealing with the risk of protectionism, and reducing poverty. Section 7 provides a summary and conclusion.

2. Trade Performance

This section examines whether China's exports have outpaced India's since reforms were initiated. Several indicators of the giants' trade and export performance are compared, including: (a) trade growth and world market shares, (b) the performance of manufactured exports according to technological categories, (c) the expansion of services exports, and (d) revealed comparative advantage at the sector level. Section 6 discusses issues of processing trade and production networks that underlie the expansion of China's exports.

Trade Growth

To trace the link between reforms and trade performance in the giants, table 1 shows the expansion of aggregate exports and imports of goods and services between 1978 and 2010. The data are from the World Bank's World Development Indicators database, and the indicators are presented as a share of gross domestic product (GDP) or world trade. The ratios of exports and imports to GDP are often used as proxies for openness, although the latter also reflects the availability of foreign exchange. Using comparable World Trade Organization (WTO) data, estimates for 2010 are also provided. To complete the picture, table 2 shows economic growth and GDP per capita in the giants. Several points about the links between reforms, trade performance, and growth are noteworthy.

Ganeshan Wignaraja

Table 1. Exports and Imports of Goods and Services, 1978–2010

	CHINA							INDIA						
	1978	1985	1991	1998	2008	2009	2010	1978	1985	1991	1998	2008	2009	2010
As % of GDP														
Exports of goods and services	6.6	9.9	20.8	20.3	36.6	26.7	31.8	6.4	5.3	8.6	11.1	22.7	20.6	22.9
Goods exports	–	8.2	15.5	18.0	33.2	24.1	25.4	4.8	4.1	6.8	8.2	16.2	12.8	15.2
Services exports	–	1.0	1.8	2.3	3.4	2.6	3.1	1.2	1.5	1.8	2.8	8.9	6.9	7.7
Imports of goods and services	7.1	14.1	17.2	16.0	28.5	22.3	28.9	6.6	7.7	8.6	12.8	28.0	25.3	30.9
Goods imports	–	12.5	13.2	13.4	24.8	19.1	25.4	5.5	6.6	7.9	10.8	27.2	18.9	22.7
Services imports	–	0.8	1.1	2.6	3.7	3.2	3.5	1.2	1.7	2.2	3.5	4.9	6.2	8.2
As % of the World														
Exports of goods and services	0.6	1.3	1.7	3.0	8.0	8.4	11.0	0.6	0.5	0.5	0.7	1.3	1.7	2.0
Goods exports	–	1.3	1.7	3.3	9.1	9.8	12.8	0.5	0.5	0.5	0.6	1.2	1.4	1.7
Services exports	–	0.7	0.8	1.7	3.8	3.7	4.9	0.6	0.8	0.5	0.8	2.7	2.6	3.2
Imports of goods and services	0.7	1.8	1.4	2.4	6.4	7.2	10.3	0.6	0.7	0.5	0.8	1.7	2.1	2.8

Table 1. Exports and Imports of Goods and Services, 1978–2010 (continued)

	CHINA							INDIA						
	1978	1985	1991	1998	2008	2009	2010	1978	1985	1991	1998	2008	2009	2010
As % of the World														
Goods imports	–	2.0	1.4	2.5	6.9	7.9	11.6	0.6	0.8	0.6	0.8	2.0	2.1	2.7
Services imports	–	0.6	0.4	1.9	4.5	4.9	5.9	0.5	0.9	0.6	1.0	1.6	2.5	3.6
Exports of goods and services (current US$, billion)	9.8	30.5	78.9	207.4	1581.7	1333.3	1748.0	8.6	12.2	23.0	46.4	262.8	269.7	326.0
Imports of goods and services (current US$, billion)	10.5	43.1	65.3	163.6	1232.8	1113.3	1587.0	9.0	17.8	23.0	53.4	324.8	330.8	440.0

Sources: For 1978–2009—World Bank, World Development Indicators, http://databank.worldbank.org, accessed April 2011; for 2010—World Trade Organization (2011).

Table 2. GDP Growth, 1960–2010 and GDP per Capita, 1978, 1991, and 2009

	CHINA	INDIA
Annual average GDP growth (constant prices, %)		
1960–1977	4.8	5.2
1978–1990	9.3	4.8
1991–2010	10.5	6.6
1960–2010	8.2	5.7
GDP per capita (current US$)		
1978	155	206
1991	330	309
2009	3,744	1,192

Sources: For 1960–2009—World Bank, World Development Indicators, http://databank.worldbank.org, accessed April 18, 2011; for 2010—Asian Development Bank, Asian Development Outlook 2011.

First, China's earlier and swifter overall trade liberalization path since 1978 compared with India's is highlighted by the ratio of exports of goods and services, and the similar ratio for imports. In 1978, China and India were at similar low levels of openness. Their exports- and imports-to-GDP ratios of 6 percent to 7 percent each reflected a history of restrictive trade regimes and state control. With increasing trade liberalization in China, its exports- and imports-to-GDP ratios

> *Trade liberalization in China caused its exports- and imports-to-GDP ratios to more than double*

more than doubled between 1978 and 1991, while India's ratios showed little change. In the aftermath of India's 1991 liberalization, a modest increase in its openness occurred between 1991 and 1998, and a significant increase took place between 1998 and 2008. China maintained its openness throughout the 1990s, and also saw a rise in exports- and imports-to-GDP ratios between 1998 and 2008. By 2008, in terms of exports (whether of goods or goods and services), China was considerably more open than

India, but there was little gap in terms of imports-to-GDP ratios. China's ratio of exports of goods and services to GDP was 36.6 percent in 2008, compared with 22.7 percent for India. Meanwhile, the ratios for imports in 2008 were similar for both countries, with 28.5 percent for China and 28 percent for India. Thus, China was relatively more open than India over several decades, but the latter has made considerable progress, particularly since the late-1990s.

Second, as China's GDP has grown faster than India's since the 1970s (see below), the trade-to-GDP ratios understate the spectacular growth of China's trade. The respective dollar values of exports and shares of world exports give a better picture of the difference in export performance between the two giants. In 1978, the two countries had about the same level of exports of goods and services, as well as similar world shares of exports: China exported $9.8 billion worth of goods and services, compared with $8.6 billion for India. These figures were equivalent to about 0.6 percent of world exports of goods and services each. By 2008, China's exports of goods and services reached a staggering $1.6 trillion, or 8.0 percent of world exports. The comparable figures for India were $263 billion and 1.3 percent.

Third, the giants' trade was relatively resilient in the wake of the global financial crisis. Following the crisis, exports of goods and services in China fell to $1.3 trillion in 2009, while India's increased slightly to $270 billion. In 2010, there were sharp rebounds in exports of goods and services to $1.8 trillion in China and $326 billion in India. Imports also rebounded to $1.6 trillion in China and $440 billion in India. Interestingly, these levels were in excess of pre-crisis

By 2010, China's exports had rebounded to $1.8 trillion, and India's to $326 billion

levels in both countries, which underscores the importance of large, dynamic domestic markets; competitive export capabilities; and the growing importance of South-South trade cooperation (Wignaraja and Lazaro 2010).

Fourth, as developed countries experienced a greater fall in exports than the giants during the global financial crisis and the sluggish response thereafter, the world export shares for China and India rose in 2010 to 11 percent and 2 percent, respectively. According to the

WTO, China's 2010 world share of exports placed it among the lead-ing exporters on the planet. The United States is the world's largest exporter (12.1 percent). China is next, followed by Germany (10.1 percent) and Japan (6.1 percent).[2] China is also the leading exporter among the so-called BRIC nations, which also includes Russia (3 percent) and Brazil (1.6 percent), as well as a comfortably placed India. Meanwhile, China's ratio of exports of goods and services to GDP rose to 31.8 percent, and India's to 22.9 percent. A similar rise was visible in the respective import-to-GDP ratios.

Fifth, increased openness and trade growth have contributed to faster economic growth of the giants. China's economic growth vir-tually doubled since the 1978 economic reforms to 9.3 percent per year (1978–1990), and still further to a staggering 10.5 percent per year (1991–2010). This compares with only 4.8 percent per year dur-ing 1960–1977. India has also experienced improved growth since the 1991 reforms, to 6.6 percent per year (1991–2010) compared with 4.4 percent (1978–1990) and 5.2 percent (1960–1977). To put such growth rates into context, the giants' annual GDP growth was well above the Organisation for Eco-nomic Co-operation and

> *Economic growth in China averaged 10.5 percent per year since 1991, and 6.6 percent in India*

Development (OECD) average in most years since the mid-1970s (see figure 1). Furthermore, growth in the giants was more robust than in OECD economies during and after the global financial crisis. Forecasts for 2011–2012 indicate a moderation of growth to above 9 percent in China and above 8 percent in India (Asian Development Bank 2011a).

Sixth, faster growth than population expansion has translated into rising per capita incomes. In 1978, China and India were considered poor, low-income economies, with India having a somewhat higher GDP per capita ($206) than China ($155). By 2009, both giants had attained the status of lower middle-income economies, but China's GDP per capita ($3,744) was over three times more than India's ($1,192). In per capita income terms, using GDP purchasing power parity (PPP) (2005 constant $), a somewhat narrower gap is visible

Figure 1. GDP Growth Rates 1975–2010

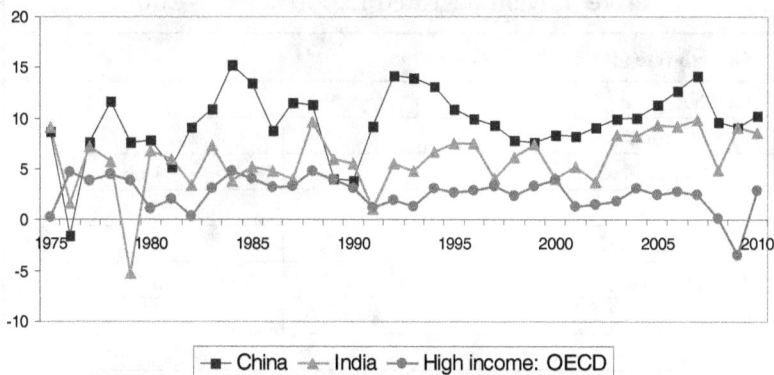

Legend: —■— China   —▲— India   —●— High income: OECD

Sources: For 1975–2009—World Bank, World Development Indicators, http://databank.worldbank.org, accessed April 18, 2011; for 2010 data of China and India—Asian Development Bank, Asian Development Outlook 2011; and for 2010 data of OECD—OECD news release, http://www.oecd.org/document/1/0,3746,en_2825_4 95684_47547073_1_1_1_1,00.html, accessed on May 12, 2011.

between the giants ($6,200 for China and $2,993 for India). Rising per capita incomes in the giants are only a crude indication of rising prosperity and may coexist amidst persistent poverty. The challenge of poverty reduction is discussed in Section 6.

Technological Upgrading in Manufactures and Rise of Services

China's exceptional export performance since 1978 has been driven primarily by the production of manufactures for export. As table 3 shows, China's manufactured export growth in current US dollars (26.7 percent) was nearly twice as fast as India's (15.4 percent) during 1985–2008. Perhaps even more strikingly, China increased its share of the world's manufactured exports from 0.5 percent to 10.8 percent between 1985 and 2008, while India's share rose from 0.5 percent to 1.3 percent over the same period.

> *China's exceptional performance since reforms has been driven by manufactured exports*

Further differences are visible between the two giants in the composition of manufactured exports. Table 3 presents United Nations

Table 3. Manufactured Exports, 1985–2008

Growth rate (1985–2008), %

CHINA	
Manufactures	26.7
Resource-based	18.6
Low tech	24.2
Medium tech	33.3
High tech	36.2
INDIA	
Manufactures	15.4
Resource-based	14.6
Low tech	13.7
Medium tech	20.2
High tec	18.3

Share of national manufactured exports, %	1985	2008
CHINA		
Resource-based	38.9	8.5
Low tech	43.7	26.8
Medium tech	12.2	37.0
High tech	5.2	27.7
INDIA		
Resource-based	40.6	35.0
Low tech	45.3	31.8
Medium tech	10.0	24.9
High tech	4.1	8.3
Share of world manufactured exports, %	**1985**	**2008**
CHINA		
Manufactures	0.5	10.8
Resource-based	0.8	3.5
Low tech	1.2	18.1
Medium tech	0.1	10.6
High tech	0.1	14.3

Share of world manufactured exports, %	1985	2008
Table 3. Manufactured Exports, 1985–2008 (continued)		
INDIA		
Manufactures	0.5	1.3
Resource-based	0.9	1.7
Low tech	1.2	2.5
Medium tech	0.1	0.8
High tech	0.1	0.5

Source: Author's calculations based on UN Comtrade, http://comtrade.un.org/, accessed December 2009.

Commodity Trade Statistics Database (UN Comtrade) information on manufactured exports for the two giants, according to a technology-based classification developed by Sanjaya Lall (2001). This method distinguishes between resource-based, low-technology, medium-technology, and high-technology manufactures. The technology categories can be briefly described as follows. Resource-based products tend to be simple and labor-intensive (e.g., simple food or leather processing), but there are segments using capital-, scale-, and skill-intensive technologies (e.g., petroleum refining or modern, processed food). Low-technology products tend to have stable, well-diffused technologies, primarily embodied in capital equipment (e.g., textiles, garments, and footwear). Medium-technology products, which consist of the majority of skill- and scale-intensive technologies in capital goods and intermediate products, lie at the core of industrial activity in developed countries. High-technology products have advanced and fast-changing technologies, with large R&D investments and a focus on product design (e.g., electronic and electrical products, aircraft, precision instruments, and pharmaceuticals). Annual average growth rates for these technological categories in current US dollars during 1985–2008, shares in manufactured exports, and shares of world exports are provided in table 3.

The following can be noted:

- Within China's manufactures, high-technology exports grew the fastest and resource-based the slowest. Meanwhile,

India's medium-technology exports grew the fastest and low-technology the slowest.

• Both giants have witnessed increasing technological up-grading of their manufactured exports since 1985, but China's speed of technological sophistication has been quite striking. Between 1985 and 2008, China's share of high-technology exports in its total manufactures increased more than five times to reach 27.7 percent in 2008. China's medium-technology exports also rose three times to 37 percent in 2008. During the same period, India's shares of high-technology exports and medium-technology exports doubled to 8.3 percent and 24.9 percent, respectively. Nonetheless, India's manufactured exports are typically concentrated in the lower end of the technology spectrum, with resource-based products accounting for one-third of manufactures and low-technology products accounting for another third.

• China has dominated world markets in low-technology products for well over a decade, and in 2008 it accounted for 18.1 percent of the world's low-technology exports. It also accounts for 10.3 percent of the world's medium-technology exports and 14.3 percent of high-technology exports. This is why China is viewed by many developing countries as the main competitive threat across the tech-nological spectrum (Lall 2001). It is also seen as an outlier in terms of the sophistication of its exports: "Its export bundle is that of a country with an income per capita level three times higher than China's" (Rodrick 2006, 4). Mean-while, India accounts for less than 1 percent of total world medium-technology and high-technology exports, and is perceived as less of a competitive threat in the developing world. Even more revealing about India's manufacturing capability is that it has a limited global presence in low-technology exports (2.5 percent in 2008) and resource-based exports (1.7 percent in 2008).

India's recent expansion in exports has been led by services rather than manufacturing. India has also kept pace with China in services export growth. A profile of India and China's service exports during 1985–2008 is shown in table 4, including growth in service exports in current US dollars, the composition of service exports by broad categories, and world market shares. India's service export grew at 16.1 percent per year compared with 18.6 percent in China during 1985–2008. In 1985, both giants were relatively small players in global service exports, with less than 1 percent of world service exports. By 2008, these shares had risen to 2.7 percent in India and 3.8 percent in

> *India's recent expansion in exports is led by services rather than manufacturing*

China. These figures may mask the area in which India has typically excelled: more sophisticated, skill-intensive services exports. India has done better in IT and business process outsourcing, as well as insurance and financial services. In 2008, India accounted for 4.7 percent of world IT and business processing outsourcing exports, compared with 4.1 percent for China. Similarly, India accounted for 1.9 percent of world insurance and financial services exports, while China's share was 0.6 percent.

Comparative Advantage at Sector Level

The revealed comparative advantage (RCA) index shows the specific sectors in which China and India are gaining or losing advantage internationally. Following Balassa (1977), the RCA index is expressed as the share of a country's exports in world trade of sector j, divided by that country's share of world trade in manufactures:

$$RCA = (X_{ij}/X_{wj})/(X_{im}/X_{wm})$$

where X_{ij} = sectoral exports from the country,
X_{wj} = sectoral exports from the world,
X_{im} = total manufactured exports from the country,
X_{wm} = total manufactured exports from the world.

Assuming that the commodity pattern of trade reflects intercountry differences in relative costs and no-price factors, this measure shows the comparative advantage of trading countries. The RCA index has a

Table 4. Commercial Services Exports, 1985–2008

Growth rate (1985–2008), %		
CHINA		
Commercial services	18.6	
Computer, communications, and other services	24.2	
Insurance and financial services	10.0	
Transport services	15.9	
Travel services	17.7	
INDIA		
Commercial services	16.1	
Computer, communications, and other services	17.4	
Insurance and financial services	23.6	
Transport services	14.3	
Travel services	11.8	
Share of national commercial service exports, %	**1985**	**2008**
CHINA		
Computer, communications, and other services	15.3	44.7
Insurance and financial services	6.7	1.2
Transport services	44.5	26.2
Travel services	33.5	27.9
INDIA		
Computer, communications, and other services	55.6	72
Insurance and financial services	1.3	5.5
Transport services	15.7	11
Travel services	27.4	11.5
Share of world commercial service exports, %	**1985**	**2008**
CHINA		
Commercial services	0.7	3.8
Computer, communications, and other services	0.4	4.1
Insurance and financial services	1.2	0.6
Transport services	1.0	4.2
Travel services	0.8	4.1

Table 4. Commercial Services Exports, 1985–2008 (continued)		
Share of world commercial service exports, %	**1985**	**2008**
INDIA		
Commercial services	0.8	2.7
Computer, communications, and other services	1.5	4.7
Insurance and financial services	0.3	1.9
Transport services	0.4	1.2
Travel services	0.7	1.2

Source: Author's calculations based on World Bank, World Development Indicators, http://databank.worldbank.org, accessed June 2010.

simple interpretation. An RCA >1 means that the sector has a larger share in world trade than the country's total manufactures and that the country has a revealed comparative advantage in that sector.

Batra and Khan (2005) have conducted one of the most comprehensive studies of sector-level revealed comparative advantage for goods exports for China and India since the adoption of reforms. Using the Balassa RCA index, they find that both countries had a comparable number of sectors (47 in China and 41 in India) with a revealed comparative advantage at the two-digit level of the Harmonized Commodity Description and Coding System (HS) classification during 2000–2003. They also report similarities in the pattern of specialization in primary products, resource-based manufactures, and labor-intensive manufactures in China and India. However, important differences emerge in science- and technology-intensive sectors. While India and China are advantageously placed in the same commodity sectors in science-based manufactures, "in absolute terms China's science-based industries are almost double the number of India" (Batra and Khan 2005, 49).

How has the pattern of revealed comparative advantage changed over time? Tables 5 and 6 show RCA indices for China and India for 2009 at the two-digit HS level. These were calculated using export data from the World Integrated Trade Solution (WITS) database. RCA estimates for goods exports in 2000 from Batra and Khan (2005) are also shown. Unfortunately, RCA indices for services exports are not available from WITS. Some comparisons are as follows.

Table 5. Sectors Where China Has Comparative Advantage [Revealed Comparative Advantage (RCA) >1], 2000 and 2009

HS code	Product, tech classification	World market share, 2009, %[a]	2009[a]		2000[b]	
			Rank (out of 44)	RCA	Rank (out of 47)	RCA
46	Manufactures of plaiting material, basketwork, etc. (LT)	71.2	1	8.0454	3	14.0000
66	Umbrellas, walking sticks, seat sticks, whips, etc. (LT)	70.1	2	7.0228	1	15.0400
67	Bird skin, feathers, artificial flowers, human hair (P)	62.9	3	6.9969	2	14.7000
50	Silk (P)	46.4	4	4.6066	4	9.6500
65	Headgear and parts thereof (LT)	42.0	5	4.4085	7	6.3200
63	Other made textile articles, sets, worn clothing, etc. (LT)	40.0	6	4.183	12	4.9800
61	Articles of apparel, accessories, knit or crochet (LT)	33.7	7	3.8745	16	4.4900
64	Footwear, gaiters and the like, parts thereof (LT)	33.6	8	3.5945	9	6.0400
58	Special woven or tufted fabric, lace, tapestry, etc. (LT)	34.6	9	3.3938	27	2.6100
42	Articles of leather, animal gut, harness, travel goods (LT)	35.3	10	3.3662	5	8.2800
95	Toys, games, sports requisites (LT)	32.4	11	3.3599	6	7.0200
62	Articles of apparel, accessories, not knit or crochet (LT)	29.7	12	3.2923	14	4.8800
60	Knitted or crocheted fabric (LT)	29.5	13	2.9969	25	2.8000
96	Miscellaneous manufactured articles (LT)	30.3	14	2.9786	22	2.9500
94	Furniture, lighting, signs, prefabricated buildings (LT)	27.0	15	2.6196	32	2.2400
52	Cotton (P)	23.2	16	2.4272	18	3.1400
92	Musical instruments, parts and accessories (LT)	23.5	17	2.4102	26	2.6200

Table 5. Sectors Where China Has Comparative Advantage [Revealed Comparative Advantage (RCA) >1], 2000 and 2009 (continued)

HS code	Product, tech classification	World market share, 2009, %[a]	2009[a]		2000[b]	
			Rank (out of 44)	RCA	Rank (out of 47)	RCA
53	Vegetable textile fibers nes, paper yarn, woven fabric (RB)	22.4	18	2.3962	13	4.9200
54	Man-made filaments (MT)	22.1	19	2.3010	44	1.1800
55	Man-made staple fibers (MT)	23.6	20	2.2968	19	3.0900
69	Ceramic products (RB)	24.3	21	2.2173	31	2.2900
59	Impregnated, coated, or laminated textile fabric (LT)	22.4	22	2.1384	n.a.	n.a.
89	Ships, boats, and other floating structures (MT)	19.7	23	1.9824	n.a.	n.a.
43	Furskins and artificial fur, manufactures thereof (LT)	22.5	24	1.9136	20	2.9800
85	Electrical, electronic equipment (HT)	18.4	25	1.9036	43	1.2200
36	Explosives, pyrotechnics, matches, pyrophorics, etc. (MT)	21.0	26	1.8795	15	4.5500
05	Products of animal origin nes (RB)	18.5	27	1.8163	10	5.5000
83	Miscellaneous articles of base metal (RB)	17.3	28	1.6366	36	1.6300
81	Other base metals, cermets, articles thereof (RB)	17.0	29	1.5832	29	2.5200
51	Wool, animal hair, horsehair yarn, and fabric thereof (P)	16.0	30	1.4933	30	2.4700
82	Tools, implements, cutlery, etc. of base metal (LT)	15.9	31	1.4650	33	2.0700
16	Meat, fish, and seafood food preparations nes (RB)	13.2	32	1.4577	21	2.9700
84	Machinery, nuclear reactors, boilers, etc. (MT/HT)	16.2	33	1.4393	n.a.	n.a.

Table 5. Sectors Where China Has Comparative Advantage [Revealed Comparative Advantage (RCA) >1], 2000 and 2009 (continued)

HS code	Product, tech classification	World market share, 2009, %[a]	2009[a]		2000[b]	
			Rank (out of 44)	RCA	Rank (out of 47)	RCA
73	Articles of iron or steel (LT)	15.2	34	1.4230	39	1.5600
68	Stone, plaster, cement, asbestos, mica, etc. articles (RB)	15.1	35	1.4072	41	1.3400
70	Glass and glassware (RB)	14.5	36	1.3880	n.a.	n.a.
57	Carpets and other textile floor coverings (LT)	12.9	37	1.3189	42	1.3200
03	Fish, crustaceans, molluscs, aquatic invertebrates nes (P)	9.8	38	1.1085	40	1.4500
56	Wadding, felt, nonwovens, yarns, twine, cordage, etc. (RB)	11.7	39	1.1034	n.a.	n.a.
20	Vegetable, fruit, nut, etc. food preparations (RB)	10.7	40	1.0935	38	1.5700
07	Edible vegetables and certain roots and tubers (P)	10.2	41	1.0882	35	1.8400
13	Lac, gums, resins, vegetable saps and extracts nes (P)	12.0	42	1.0429	n.a.	n.a.
86	Railway, tramway locomotives, rolling stock, equipment (MT)	11.2	43	1.0227	11	5.1300
14	Vegetable plaiting materials, vegetable products nes (RB)	8.6	44	1.0027	28	2.5300

Sources:
[a]Estimates from World Bank, World Integrated Trade Solution, http://wits.worldbank.org/wits/, accessed April 2011.
[b]Estimates from Batra and Khan (2005) using the Balassa RCA index method.

Notes: n.a. = RCA rank not available from Batra and Khan (2005), but likely that product has RCA<1; technology-based classification using Lall (2001): P = primary, RB = resource-based manufactures, LT = low-technology manufactures, MT = medium-technology manufactures, HT = high-technology manufactures.

Table 6. Sectors Where India Has Comparative Advantage [Revealed Comparative Advantage (RCA) >1], 2000 and 2009

HS code	Product, tech classification	World market share, 2009, %[a]	2009[a]		2000[b]	
			Rank (out of 37)	RCA	Rank (out of 42)	RCA
71	Pearls, precious stones, metals, coins, etc. (RB)	10.2	1	7.4000	6	9.1800
50	Silk (P)	9.8	2	6.5937	2	16.4300
57	Carpets and other textile floor coverings (LT)	8.5	3	5.8813	4	9.9800
52	Cotton (P)	7.7	4	5.4905	3	11.3400
13	Lac, gums, resins, vegetable saps and extracts nes (P)	8.4	5	4.9454	1	17.0100
53	Vegetable textile fibers nes, paper yarn, woven fabric (RB)	6.5	6	4.6826	8	7.5700
26	Ores, slag, and ash (RB)	5.0	7	4.1648	24	2.4300
14	Vegetable plaiting materials, vegetable products nes (RB)	5.1	8	4.0449	10	6.1000
63	Other made textile articles, sets, worn clothing, etc. (LT)	5.5	9	3.9220	5	9.2800
67	Bird skin, feathers, artificial flowers, human hair (P)	5.1	10	3.8659	13	3.9000
09	Coffee, tea, mate, and spices (P)	5.1	11	3.7800	7	8.3500
54	Man-made filaments (MT)	5.3	12	3.7222	22	2.5600
55	Man-made staple fibers (MT)	4.7	13	3.1297	18	3.0600
62	Articles of apparel, accessories, not knit or crochet (LT)	3.9	14	2.9342	11	5.4800
10	Cereals (P)	3.9	15	2.8040	19	2.9700
61	Articles of apparel, accessories, knit or crochet (LT)	3.2	16	2.5413	16	3.3400
79	Zinc and articles thereof (RB)	3.6	17	2.5257	n.a.	n.a.
25	Salt, sulphur, earth, stone, plaster, lime, and cement (RB)	3.3	18	2.3930	15	3.6700

Table 6. Sectors Where India Has Comparative Advantage [Revealed Comparative Advantage (RCA) >1], 2000 and 2009 (continued)

HS code	Product, tech classification	World market share, 2009, %[a]	2009[a]		2000[b]	
			Rank (out of 37)	RCA	Rank (out of 42)	RCA
23	Residues, wastes of food industry, animal fodder (RB)	3.4	19	2.3592	17	3.1300
42	Articles of leather, animal gut, harness, travel goods (LT)	3.3	20	2.1459	9	7.1600
99	Commodities not elsewhere specified (LT)	1.4	21	2.0047	n.a.	n.a.
89	Ships, boats, and other floating structures (MT)	2.6	22	1.7879	n.a.	n.a.
41	Raw hides and skins (other than fur) and leather (P)	2.7	23	1.7713	21	2.7400
24	Tobacco and manufactured tobacco substitutes (RB)	2.6	24	1.7614	36	1.2400
68	Stone, plaster, cement, asbestos, mica, etc. articles (RB)	2.6	25	1.6639	23	2.5100
03	Fish, crustaceans, mollusks, aquatic invertebrates nes (P)	2.0	26	1.5621	12	4.9100
29	Organic chemicals (RB)	2.4	27	1.4462	31	1.5700
64	Footwear, gaiters and the like, parts thereof (LT)	1.8	28	1.2919	26	2.2000
32	Tanning, dyeing extracts, tannins, derivs, pigments, etc. (RB)	2.1	29	1.2798	27	1.9800
27	Mineral fuels, oils, distillation products, etc. (RB)	1.4	30	1.2738	n.a.	n.a.
36	Explosives, pyrotechnics, matches, pyrophorics, etc. (MT)	2.1	31	1.2671	39	1.1800
58	Special woven or tufted fabric, lace, tapestry, etc. (LT)	1.9	32	1.2661	14	3.8700
73	Articles of iron or steel (LT)	1.9	33	1.2282	30	1.6200
07	Edible vegetables and certain roots and tubers (P)	1.7	34	1.2160	28	1.7700

Table 6. Sectors Where India Has Comparative Advantage [Revealed Comparative Advantage (RCA) >1], 2000 and 2009 (continued)

HS code	Product, tech classification	World market share, 2009, %[a]	2009[a]		2000[b]	
			Rank (out of 37)	RCA	Rank (out of 42)	RCA
08	Edible fruit, nuts, peel of citrus fruit, melons (P)	1.5	35	1.1570	20	2.9200
72	Iron and steel (RB)	1.6	36	1.1133	34	1.2900
74	Copper and articles thereof (RB)	1.5	37	1.0243	n.a.	n.a.

Sources:
[a]Estimates from World Bank, World Integrated Trade Solution, http://wits.worldbank.org/wits/, accessed April 2011.
[b]Estimates from Batra and Khan (2005) using the Balassa RCA index method.
Notes: n.a. = RCA rank not available from Batra and Khan (2005), but likely that product has RCA<1; technology-based classification using Lall (2001): P = primary, RB = resource-based manufactures, LT = low-technology manufactures, MT = medium-technology manufactures, HT = high-technology manufactures.

The evidence suggests that China's comparative advantage at the sector level appears more robust than India's. The number of sectors with a revealed comparative advantage (RCA) in both countries is approximately the same between 2000 and 2009. But in 2009, China still had more sectors with a RCA than India and more visible relative strength in manufactured exports, particularly medium- and high-technology products. Out of 97 at the HS two-digit level, China had 44 sectors with an RCA index of above one in 2009, while India had only 37.

Low-technology manufactured products dominate China's top ten sectors, according to RCA indices. Manufactures of plaiting material (HS 46) and of umbrellas, walking sticks, and seat sticks (HS 66) are the two top-ranked RCA sectors in China. Also prominent in China are artificial flowers, human hair, headgear, textiles, apparel, footwear, and leather articles. In contrast, India's top 10 RCAs comprise a mix of primary products, resource-based manufactures, and some low-technology manufactures. India's top two sectors are pearls, precious stones, metals, and coins (HS 71) and silk (HS 50). These are followed by carpets, other textile flooring, cotton, lac, gums, vegetable textile fibers, paper yarn, woven fabric, ores, slag, ash, vegetable plaiting materials, vegetable products, other textiles, bird skin, and feathers.

Furthermore, as indicated above, a growing divergence has occurred between the giants in medium-technology and high-technology products since 2000 in the pattern of specialization, as well as in absolute terms. Some examples tell the story. A crucial high-technology manufactured product like electrical and electronics products (HS 85) jumped from 43 to 25 in China's RCA rankings between 2000 and 2009, but is not visible in India's list of 37 products with an RCA of above 1. And China had an impressive world market share of 18.4 percent in electrical and electronics products in 2009. Another example is ships, boats, and floating structures (a medium-technology product). Here, China and India are ranked at 23 and 22 in their respective RCA lists. However, China controlled one-fifth of the world market in ships, boats, and floating structures, while India had only 2.6 percent. Similar tales are visible in other medium- and high-technology products, including machinery, nuclear reactors, boilers, explosives, pyrotechnics, iron, and steel. Interestingly, China's RCA ranking in railway products and equipment slipped from 11 to 43 between 2000 and 2009, but it retains an 11.2 percent world market share. India enjoys some success in organic chemicals, which increased from 31 to 27, with a world market share of 2.4 percent.

Thus, the giants have differed considerably in their trade performance since the reforms. China has surged ahead of India in world export markets, with China's exports of goods and services over five times bigger than India's. China's success is linked to the rise of manufactured exports, which have rapidly upgraded over time, and to the expansion of some services. Strong revealed comparative advantages in a host of medium- and high-technology manufactured sectors are visible in China. Meanwhile, India has done better in skill-intensive services than manufactures. Compared with developed countries, the giants' export performances have been relatively resilient since the global financial crisis. Reforms and trade expansion have resulted in faster economic growth and rising GDP per capita over time.

3. Role of Initial Conditions

The outcome of economic reforms on trade performance is shaped by initial conditions (e.g., geography, market size, and institutions) in the country implementing it. Typically, countries with favorable geography, market size, and institutions seem to perform better than others following economic reforms. A detailed assessment of how trade outcomes are related to initial conditions in China and India is beyond the

> *Economic reforms work in tandem with favorable geography, market size, and institutions*

scope of this paper. Nonetheless, it is worth highlighting four key initial conditions that appear to have influenced the trade pattern and performance of the giants after the implementation of reforms.

One is that geographical proximity to a major developed economy can result in spillovers for neighbors. China's strategic location in East Asia and shared history meant that it was well placed to attract export-oriented manufacturing FDI from Japan, South Korea, Hong Kong, Taiwan, and economies forming the Association of Southeast Asian Nations (ASEAN). Geographical proximity, along with low-cost labor and large market size, may have also influenced the relocation of production networks and supply chains from ASEAN economies to China. India is less well-placed geographically for attracting FDI from East Asia, but is closer to Europe than China and shares greater ties due to its legacy of British rule.

The second initial condition is the presence of large and growing domestic markets that create a competitive advantage for any product that has substantial economies of scale (e.g., automobile or electronics assembly) and lower barriers to entry. So how large are the Chinese and Indian markets? Population data can be misleading as an indication of market size as they show the giants being quite similar—China with 1.3 billion people in 2010 and India with 1.2 billion. More useful are GDP-based estimates of market size. It is estimated that industrial producers in China face a potential market of about $1 trillion, while India's industrial producers face a potential market that is one-quarter to one-third of China's size (Yusuf, Nabeshima, and Perkins 2007).

The third condition is an ample supply of low-cost, productive manpower to provide the basis for a comparative advantage in low-technology, labor-intensive exports and to attract FDI. It is often suggested by various competitiveness studies that China's labor productivity is higher than India's and that this advantage underlies China's entry into labor-intensive manufactures (World Economic Forum 2010). Meanwhile, the roots of India's relative success in IT and business process outsourcing lie in other factors, including its exposure to English that is linked to a long period of British colonial rule; the establishment of Indian Institutes of Technology, which provided a base of world-class IT professionals and engineers; close links with a diaspora of professionals and business people who provided relevant contacts, information, and capital; and falling telecommunications costs, which made it profitable to outsource services (Yusuf, Nabeshima, and Perkins 2007; Kowalski 2010).

Fourth, myriad institutions are likely to be relevant in explaining trade outcomes following reforms in China and India. The role of township and village enterprises (TVEs) in Chinese industry since the reforms has attracted interest in the literature. TVEs, largely under the control of local governments, led labor-intensive, rural industrialization in China, and they became the most vibrant part of the Chinese economy in the 1980s and early 1990s. The share of TVEs in GDP jumped from 6 percent to 26 percent between 1978 and 1996 (Bardhan 2010, 20). In provinces like Jiangsu and Shandong, TVEs employed as much as 30 percent of the rural labor force. Their success is attributed to the following: some crowding out of private enterprises in the early years of reform as a legacy of pre-reform policies; fiscal decentralization and greater decision-making powers to local government officials, which provided incentives to promote TVEs; pent-up demand for consumer products, including those produced by TVEs; and loans from state banks (Huang 2008). After the mid-1990s, however, TVEs declined with market development privatization and more FDI. Thus, TVEs were an important institutional vehicle for mass industrialization and export-led growth in China.

While India has a significant base of small firms that account for a high proportion of industrial employment, the jury is still out as to whether they have played a similar role in spurring rural industrialization and exports as did Chinese TVEs. There are cases of successful small Indian firms in labor-intensive manufactures and IT-linked services. However, it is argued that small firms in India are typically constrained by several issues (e.g., plagued by technical inefficiency, shielded from foreign competition, hamstrung by procedural impediments, and lacking sufficient access to finance) that have hampered their performance in the post-1991 period (see, for instance, Panagariya 2007). Accordingly, large firms account for much of Indian manufacturing production and exports. Using firm-level data, Srinivasan and Archana (2011) attempt to model and estimate the decision of Indian firms on their participation in trade. Firm heterogeneity is an important determinant of the decision to export in Indian firms. Srinivasan and Archana found that exporting firms are significantly larger, more R&D intensive, low-wage intensive, more productive, and more profitable than non-exporting firms.

Trade outcomes since reforms were enacted have broadly been influenced by initial conditions in the giants, with such conditions in China appearing somewhat more favorable than those in India. Nevertheless, initial conditions alone cannot account for the whole export story in China and India. The timing, content, and sequencing of economic reforms have also played a major role in facilitating specialization and trade. We turn to this topic next.

Timing, content, and sequencing of economic reforms also play major roles

4. Anatomy of Trade and Investment Reforms

The central question of this paper concerns the role that liberalization of trade and investment regimes has played in the giants' export records. This section focuses on key changes in trade and investment policies—import liberalization, export-promotion measures, and FDI policies—at the heart of China's and India's reforms. An attempt is made to assess the incentive effect of individual reforms on private sector export behavior, as well as the net incentive effect. The giants are considered separately below, followed by some comparisons of their reforms and export outcomes. Table 7 provides an overview of trade and investment policies during the era of reform.

Table 7. Key Trade and Investment Policies
During the Reform Era

CHINA	INDIA

Attracting export-oriented FDI
• Passage of an export processing law (1979).
• Adoption of a dualistic trade regime that promoted exports via FDI (mid-1980s).
• Easing of regulations on the entry and operation of foreign enterprises (through the Sino-Foreign Equity Joint Venture Law of 1979, Sino-Foreign Cooperative Joint Venture Law of 1986, and the Wholly Foreign-Owned Enterprise Law of 1988).
• Creation of Special Economic Zones (SEZs) (1980s).
  • Introduction of tax incentives and facilitation of financing to channel FDI towards SEZs.
  • Liberalization of labor regulations in SEZs ensuring relatively low wages and ample supply of skilled workers.
• Formalization of a duty drawback system to ensure duty-free access to materials used in export processing (1987 onwards).
	• Gradual liberalization of restrictions on foreign ownership through a system of automatic clearance for FDI proposals and the opening up of new sectors to foreign ownership (e.g., mining, software, banking, telecommunications) (1991 onwards).
	• Formal FDI Policy adopted (1996).
	• 100% foreign ownership permitted in most manufacturing sectors (late-1990s).
	• Passage of a Special Economic Zones Act to promote exports more systematically with incentives (2005).

Import liberalization • Passage of a customs regulation to rationalize tariff schedules (1985). • Liberalization of the system of export licensing and quotas (from covering 2/3 of exports in 1991 to only 8% in 1999). • Tariff reductions implemented following the adoption of a socialist market (1992 onwards). • Further reforms to import control regime implemented as part of WTO accession (2001).	• Introduction of a package of trade and investment reforms (1991). • Abolition of import licensing on machinery and raw materials (1991). • Establishment of India, as signatory to the General Agreement on Tariffs and Trade (GATT), as a founding member of the WTO (January 1, 1995). • Abolition of licensing on consumer goods (2001).

Table 7. Key Trade and Investment Policies During the Reform Era (continued)	
CHINA	**INDIA**
Exchange rate management • Devaluation of domestic currency and movement to currency convertibility of account transactions (1997). • Adoption of a managed floating exchange rate (mid-2005 onwards)	• Unification of the dual exchange rate system and commencement of current account convertibility (1994). • Maintenance of a depreciated exchange rate (2000 onwards).
FTA strategies • Accession to its first FTA, the Asia-Pacific Trade Agreement (2001). • Signing of the ASEAN-China FTA (2005). • Establishment of 11 FTAs, including bilateral agreements with Thailand, Hong Kong, Macao, Chile, New Zealand, Pakistan, Singapore, Peru, and Taipei (as of June 2011).	• Signing of its first FTA, the Asia-Pacific Trade Agreement (1976). • Signing of the South Asian FTA (2006). • Establishment of 11 FTAs, including bilateral agreements with Sri Lanka, Nepal, Afghanistan, Singapore, Bhutan, Chile, South Korea, and a plurilateral agreement with Latin American countries (as of June 2011).

China's Approach to Economic Reforms

Inward-Oriented Strategy

China initiated reforms in 1978 to shift to a more open, market-oriented economy. The previous inward-oriented, centrally planned strategy had caused multiple economic distortions that hampered exports and private sector activity. The inward-oriented strategy, introduced in the 1950s, fostered import-substituting industrialization using stringent protection and state control of resource allocation. During the Maoist period, private sector firms, including foreign-owned firms, were gradually taken over, and private sector ownership was completely eliminated in 1958 during the Great Leap Forward. Instead, state-owned enterprises emerged at the forefront of the country's industrialization effort. A formal state-owned enterprise sector made up of large firms and a proletarian elite of workers with job security and generous welfare benefits coexisted with less-capitalized, small-scale industrial enterprises based mainly in rural areas, where workers enjoyed less security and benefits (Maddison 2007).

Some of the economic distortions that arose from China's inward-oriented strategy were as follows:

1. Stringent quantitative restrictions and other import controls led to a bias toward inefficient capital-intensive production by large, state-owned enterprises.

2. The exchange rate was fixed at an overvalued level to implicitly subsidize the import of high-priority capital goods that could not be produced domestically. A rigid system of exchange control also existed, whereby exporters surrendered all their foreign exchange to the state.

3. Foreign direct investment (FDI) and technology transfer were shut out by tight controls on the entry of foreign enterprises, resulting in technological obsolescence relative to global best practices.

4. Virtually all commodity trade was determined by central planning, primarily to ensure that state-owned enterprises could obtain cheap imports of capital goods and intermediates. A handful of foreign trade cooperatives owned and controlled by the Ministry of Foreign Trade was responsible for carrying out the trade plan. Each of the foreign trade cooperatives dealt with a limited range of commodities, for which it was the sole trading company.

Not surprisingly, owing to these inefficiencies and distortions, China witnessed lackluster export performance during much of the inward-oriented, centrally planned era. By 1978, China had developed a large manufacturing sector behind high tariff walls and state controls, accounting for 41 percent of GDP. However, its exports of goods and services had stagnated at less than $10 billion (or 0.6 percent of world exports of goods and services) in 1978. The composition of exports was dominated by primary products, resource-based manufactures, and some low-technology manufactures. The time was ripe for a change in policies toward export promotion and the private sector.

Trade and Investment Reforms

The post-1978 reforms marked the start of a gradual and highly coordinated transition process in China over the next three decades. The initial focus of reforms was to promote exports by attracting FDI. In 1979, an export-processing law was passed that provided incentives for the processing and assembly of imported inputs. These incentives were expanded in 1987 to provide for the duty-free import of all raw materials, parts, and components used in export production. Monopoly state trading was liberalized starting in the late-1970s and replaced with a complex and highly restrictive set of tariffs, nontariff barriers, and licenses. Reform of the complex import control regime was more cautious during the early transition years, but was strengthened from 1992 onward by extensive reforms that China agreed to implement as part of the WTO accession process. Accordingly, a dualistic trade regime existed from the mid-1980s onward, one that promoted exports via FDI alongside controlled liberalization of a protected domestic sector (Kowalski 2010).

China instituted gradual and highly coordinated reforms over three decades

To attract export-oriented FDI, China implemented five main measures beginning in the late-1970s (Zhang 2009). These included the following:

1. Regulations governing the entry and operation of foreign enterprises were eased through a series of laws, notably the Sino-Foreign Equity Joint Venture Law of 1979, Sino-Foreign Cooperative Joint Venture Law of 1986, and the Wholly Foreign-Owned Enterprise Law of 1988. Such measures encouraged the formation of joint ventures between foreign and local investors, technology transfer to local partners, and domestic sourcing of inputs. In later years, measures were introduced to facilitate the operation of wholly foreign-owned enterprises.

2. Efficient, cost-competitive infrastructure for export processing commenced with four special economic zones (SEZs) along China's southern coast. These zones enabled foreign producers to operate with good infrastructure and a minimum of undue interference.

3. A complex system of tax incentives (including a 15 percent corporation tax rate, exemptions, and refunds) and facilitation of financing were introduced to channel FDI towards the SEZs.

4. A duty drawback system was formalized from 1987 onward to ensure duty-free access to all imported raw materials, parts, and components for export processing.

5. Liberal labor regulations in SEZs were applied to ensure relatively low wages for ample supplies of skilled workers.

Two other policies were vital to export growth, especially among domestic enterprises (Lardy 2003). First, the system of export licensing and quotas was liberalized. By 1999, only 8 percent of exports were subject to export licensing and quotas, compared to a peak in 1991 where some two-thirds of all exports were so burdened.

Second, reforms of the foreign exchange system were initiated starting with the unification of dual exchange rates in 1994 (Hu 2010). As a significant incentive for exporting, exporters were allowed to retain a share of their foreign exchange earnings, which enabled them to finance imports without needing to seek official permission. Over time, the state also devalued the domestic currency and, in 1997, moved to currency convertibility on current account transactions, making it even easier for exporters to obtain foreign currency. In mid-2005, China moved more systematically toward a managed floating exchange rate regime, one that was based on market supply and demand with reference to a basket of currencies.

Despite the various measures to attract FDI and promote exports, FDI inflows were modest in the first decade or so of reforms. As table 8 shows, annual average FDI inflows amounted to $1.6 billion a year during 1978–1990 and were largely destined for the four SEZs.

Table 8. Foreign Direct Investment (FDI), 1978–2010
(current US$, billion)

	CHINA	INDIA
Total FDI inflows (current US$, billion) 1978–2010	1098.7	191.3
Annual average FDI inflows (current US$, billion)		
1978–1990	1.6	0.1
1991–2010	54.0	9.5
1991–2002	35.6	2.5
2003–2010	81.5	20.0
2008	108.3	41.6
2009	95.0	34.6
2010	105.7[a]	21.0[b]
FDI inflows (% of GDP)		
1991–1995	3.8	0.2
2004–2010	2.6	2.0
2008	2.4	3.4
2009	2.0	2.8
2010	1.9	1.5
Share of multinational companies in exports (%), most recent estimate[c]	55	<10
Total outward FDI (current US$, billion) 1995–2009	182.0	73.1
Annual average outward FDI (current US$, billion)		
1995–2005	3.8	1.0
2006–2009	38.6	16.7
2008	52.2	18.5
2009	48.0	14.9

Sources: Author's calculations based on data from UNCTAD, UNCTADStat, http://unctadstat.unctad.org/, accessed April 2011.

[a]Estimates from the Government of the People's Republic of China–Ministry of Commerce, http://english.mofcom.gov.cn/aarticle/statistic/foreigninvestment/201101/20110107381641.html. accessed April 2011.

[b]Estimates from the Government of India–Ministry of Commerce and Industry, http://dipp.nic.in/fdi_statistics/india_FDI_December2010.pdf, accessed April 2011.

[c]Estimates from Kumar and Sharma (2009).

From the early 1990s onward, however, China attracted record levels of FDI, with inflows amounting to $54 billion per year during 1991–2010. Annual FDI inflows in 2003–2010 ($81.5 billion) were more than double that of the 1991–2002 period. Cumulative FDI inflows into China reached an impressive $1,098.7 billion in 1978–2010. As a result, China became the world's second largest FDI recipient after the United States. Interestingly, the global financial crisis did not significantly disrupt FDI inflows, which dropped modestly from a peak $108.3 billion in 2008 to $95 billion in 2009. FDI inflows rebounded to pre-crisis levels in 2010 ($105.7 billion).

A strong regional element is visible in the host country origin of China's FDI inflows. Much of the surge in FDI inflows into China since the 1990s has come from overseas Chinese investors—primarily based in Hong Kong, Taiwan, and Macao—who collectively accounted for 42 percent of accumulated FDI inflows during 1997–2006 (Zhang 2009). Another 21.2 percent of FDI inflows was from other East Asian countries, primarily Japan, South Korea, and ASEAN members.

> *Surging FDI inflows into China come mostly from Chinese investors in Hong Kong, Taipei, and Macao*

Among nonregionals, the United States made up 7.8 percent and the European Union (EU) 8.6 percent. Interestingly, the share of overseas Chinese investors rose significantly to 56.9 percent in 2008. Meanwhile, the shares of other East Asian countries (17.3 percent), the EU (6.7 percent) and the United States (6.4 percent) declined somewhat (Government of the People's Republic of China-Ministry of Commerce 2011).

The infusion of FDI had a dramatic impact on China's exports. The share of foreign enterprises in total Chinese exports increased from 32 percent to 58 percent between 1995 and 2005, and then declined slightly to 54 percent in 2010 (January to August).[3] Inflows of FDI have been fundamental to China's success in manufactured exports by linking the country into production networks in key industries. FDI brought not only capital, but, more importantly, access to marketing channels, world-class technologies, and organizational methods. In the early years of reforms, FDI was central to the rise of low-technology, labor-intensive exports, such as textiles, garments, and footwear. Subsequently, the surge in FDI in the 1990s drove the rapid technological upgrading of manufactures into more complex activities, such as electronics and automotives. Recent micro-level studies have analyzed the relationship between imported technology (via FDI and foreign buyers) and innovation and learning in Chinese manufacturing enterprises (e.g., electronics, automotives, and textiles). The evidence indicates that technology transfer from abroad was complemented by systematic investments in technological capabilities to use imported technologies efficiently, as well as upgrading of technical skills (see Wignaraja 2008 and 2011). Hence, FDI and domestic technological activity underlie China's export success.

Research also suggests that China used active policies to facilitate technology upgrading and domestic technological development. Entry and operational regulations for foreign firms required them to form joint ventures with domestic firms, promote technology transfer to partners, and increase local content by sourcing inputs locally (Rodrick 2006). The authorities at central and regional levels also promoted quality upgrades in China's product structure using tax and other policy incentives. These incentives were often formalized in the spread of export processing zones and high-tech industrial zones around China (Feenstra and Wei 2010). Furthermore, China invested heavily in R&D and in scientists and engineers to absorb imported technologies. Its R&D expenditure to GDP ratio more than doubled, from 0.6 percent to 1.5 percent between 1996 and 2007 (see table 13). Researchers in R&D per million also doubled, from 448 to 1,071 during this period.

More recently, China has become a notable outward investor in the world economy (see table 8). During 1995–2005, annual outward FDI from China was relatively small at $3.8 billion per year. Such flows increased more than five-fold to about $22 billion in 2006–2007, and peaked at $52.2 billion in 2008 on the eve of the global financial crisis. Following the crisis, there was a modest drop in China's outward investment to about $48 billion in 2009. The bulk of outward FDI has been into the primary and tertiary sectors, with relatively little, so far, going into manufacturing (Davies 2010). Most has gone to Asia, but Chinese FDI is now spreading throughout the world. In part, the growth of outward FDI reflects a combination of large export surpluses, rising wages, a global search for commodities to fuel industrialization, and the emergence of large, homegrown multi-national corporations looking for overseas investment opportunities.

Import Liberalization, WTO Accession, and Exchange Rates
The liberalization of import controls began slowly and cautiously in China from the early 1980s onward.[4] In part, this was to permit state-owned enterprises and township and village enterprises (TVEs) time to adjust to import competition (Huang 2008). Two parallel stages in import liberalization can be identified that led to significant cuts in overall import protection over time. First, in an effort to move away from the direct planning of all trade, a simplified system of import quotas and licensing was adopted in the early 1980s, and the number of products under import controls was reduced. The share of imports under quotas and licensing fell from 46 percent to 18 percent between the late 1980s and 1992, and fell still further to about 9 percent in 1997 (Lardy 2002, 39). Second, more transparent price-based instruments—import tariffs—were introduced in the early 1980s to replace quotas and licenses, and tariff reduction subsequently commenced. In 1985, a new customs regulation was passed which rationalized the tariff schedule. More notable tariff cuts occurred following the adoption of a socialist market economy in 1992.

The process of tariff reduction was also facilitated by the significant reforms that the country agreed to implement as part of its accession to the WTO in 2001. Achieved after 14 years of difficult negotiations with GATT (General Agreement on Tariffs and Trade)/WTO members—which included China agreeing to significant reductions in agricultural tariffs—China's WTO membership was hailed as a major milestone in the development of the Chinese economy and the multilateral trading system. Membership in the WTO was thought to bring numerous benefits, such as a deepened integration of the Chinese economy into the global economy, increased trade and investment, and easier dispute settlement via a rules-based international trading system.

> **WTO membership was a major milestone in the development of the Chinese economy**

China generally followed through on its liberalization commitments made during WTO accession and unilateral reforms. The available tariff data indicate an overall move toward a more open and transparent import regime. Simple, average tariffs on all imports fell modestly, from 55.6 percent to 43.2 percent between 1982 and 1992 (Lardy 2002, 34). Thereafter, the pace of tariff reform accelerated. Table 9 provides data from the WTO Integrated Database and the WTO Tariff Profiles on simple, average, applied most-favored nation (MFN) tariffs for agricultural products, nonagricultural products, and total products between 1996 and 2009. Average import tariffs fell to 23.7 percent in 1996, and still further to 15.9 percent on the eve of WTO accession in 2001. The continuing process of tariff reduction resulted in average import tariffs of 9.6 percent by 2009. Accordingly, China became one of the more open economies in the developing world. Nonagricultural products typically enjoyed less tariff protection than agricultural products and experienced swifter tariff reduction. In 1996, average import tariffs for nonagricultural products (22.8 percent) were significantly lower than those for agricultural products (34.1 percent). By 2009, import tariffs for nonagricultural products reached 8.7 percent, and those for agricultural products were 15.6 percent.

Table 10 provides the latest data on MFN-applied tariffs and imports by product groups for 2009. There is relatively little dispersion in import tariffs for nonagricultural products, which range from 4.4 percent for wood and paper to 16 percent for clothing. Within this general picture, major high-technology products have lower tariffs than less dynamic low-technology products. Thus, import tariffs for electrical machinery, for nonelectrical machinery, and transport equipment are respectively 8.0 percent, 7.8 percent, and 11.5 percent.

Table 9. Simple Average Applied MFN Tariffs, by Broad Sectors, 1996, 2001, 2008, and 2009

	CHINA				INDIA			
	1996	2001	2008	2009	1996	2001	2008	2009
All	23.7	15.9	9.6	9.6	38.7	31.9	13	12.9
Agricultural products	34.1	20.3	15.6	15.6	23.1	36.3	32.2	31.8
Nonagricultural products	22.8	15.5	8.7	8.7	40.1	31.4	10.1	10.1

Source: Author's calculations based on data from UNCTAD, UNCTADStat, http://unctadstat.unctad.org/, accessed April 2011.

Table 10. MFN-Applied Tariffs and Share of Imports,
by Product, 2009

Product groups	CHINA			INDIA		
	MFN-applied duties		Imports	MFN-applied duties		Imports
	AVG	Max	Share, %	AVG	Max	Share, %
Animal products	14.8	25	0.2	33.1	100	0.0
Dairy products	12.0	20	0.1	33.7	60	0.0
Fruit, vegetables, plants	14.8	30	0.2	30.4	100	0.9
Coffee, tea	14.7	32	0.0	56.3	100	0.1
Cereals and preparations	24.2	65	0.2	32.2	150	0.0
Oilseeds, fats, and oils	10.9	30	3.3	18.2	100	1.3
Sugars and confectionery	27.4	50	0.0	34.4	60	0.1
Beverages and tobacco	22.9	65	0.2	70.8	150	0.1
Cotton	15.2	40	0.3	12.0	30	0.1
Other agricultural products	11.5	38	0.5	21.7	70	0.3
Fish and fish products	10.7	23	0.5	29.8	30	0.0
Minerals and metals	7.4	50	18.8	7.5	10	33.3
Petroleum	4.4	9	15.4	3.8	5	29.1
Chemicals	6.6	47	11.3	7.9	10	7.5
Wood, paper, etc.	4.4	20	2.5	9.1	10	1.6
Textiles	9.6	38	1.5	13.6	246	0.9
Clothing	16.0	25	0.2	16.1	68	0.0
Leather, footwear, etc.	13.4	25	1.6	10.2	70	0.7
Nonelectrical machinery	7.8	35	11.8	7.3	10	9.1
Electrical machinery	8.0	35	20.1	7.2	10	7.7
Transport equipment	11.5	45	3.8	20.7	100	4.5
Manufactures, nes	11.9	35	7.3	8.9	10	2.6

Source: World Trade Organization, WTO Statistics Database–Tariff Profiles, http://stat.wto.org/TariffProfile
/WSDBTariffPFHome.aspx?Language=E, accessed April 2011.

This compares with import tariffs of 16 percent for clothing and 13.4 percent for leather and footwear. In contrast, a larger dispersion in import tariffs is visible for agricultural products, from 10.6 percent for oilseeds, fats, and oils to 27.4 percent for sugars and confectionary.

At the same time, however, some have expressed concerns that China's WTO accession has resulted in more challenges to China, its trading partners, and the WTO itself. Key issues are whether more trade disputes have arisen since China's WTO accession and if the WTO's relatively new dispute-settlement mechanism has been over-stretched. Recent research (e.g., Bowen 2010) reports some interesting findings. Before 2001, China exporters were more likely to face antidumping charges than exporters from other countries. After 2001, there seems to be an increase in antidumping investigations against Chinese exports by, for example, both the United States and the European Union. China invested significantly in learning about the WTO dispute-settlement mechanism and preparing to actively respond to cases against itself, as well as in initiating cases against trading partners. Subsequently, China appears to have become a leading user of antidumping investigations internationally, possibly associated with industries that had the biggest reductions in tariffs during WTO accession. Nonetheless, the risk of overwhelming the capacity of the WTO dispute-settlement mechanism has not materialized.

Exchange rate management has assumed more significance for exporting from China since the turn of the millennium. In essence, the People's Bank of China has pursued a managed, floating-exchange regime whereby the renminbi exchange rate is based on the supply and demand of the market, and adjusted with reference to a basket of currencies (Hu 2010). A key policy objective is to maintain a relatively stable and predictable nominal exchange rate of the renminbi. A standard measure of international competitiveness is the real effective exchange rate (REER)—the weighted average of a country's currency relative to an index or basket of other major currencies, adjusted for the effects of inflation. Figure 2 charts monthly Bank for International Settlements (BIS) data on the REER for China from January 2000 to May 2011. The base year for the REER series is 2005. The REER exhibits a U-shaped pattern during this period. After a short initial appreciation between January 2000 and April 2002, the REER remained depreciated between May 2002 and December 2007. Thereafter, the

Figure 2. Real Effective Exchange Rate of China and India,
January 2000–May 2011 (monthly)

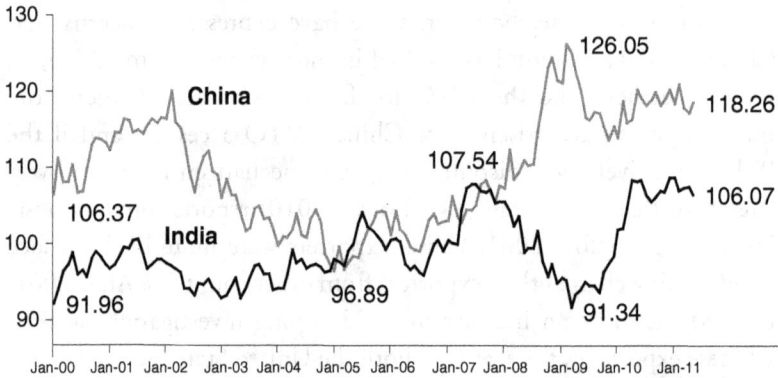

Source: Author's calculations based on data from the Bank for International Settlements,
http://www.bis.org/, accessed June 2011.
Notes: Consumer price index (CPI)–based, 2005 = 100; increase = appreciation.

REER behaved somewhat erratically, with an appreciating tendency.
Thus, for much of the last decade, China's inflation was below that
of its trading partners, and the rate of nominal exchange depreciation
was sufficient to offset this inflation differential. Section 6 analyzes
recent developments in exchange rate management in the context of
China-US economic relations.

India's Approach to Economic Reforms

Inward-Oriented Strategy
The start of import substitution in India in the late-1950s introduced policy interventions on trade and developed into one of the
most highly protected and inward-oriented regimes in the developing world. The regime continued,
with some minor changes, into
the 1980s. Popular discourse often
equates India's reforms, especially
of trade and investment policies,
with the post-1991 period. Partial
reforms, however, were attempted

> *1950s trade policies turned
> India into a highly protected,
> inward-oriented regime*

in the previous decade. Accordingly, three phases can be identified in the history of India's reforms: (1) inward-oriented, state-controlled policies (1950–1975); (2) partial liberalization (1976–1991), particularly since the mid-1980s; and (3) major reforms from 1991 onwards (Panagariya 2004).

During the first and second phases, balance of payments pressures in the 1950s led to comprehensive import controls to conserve foreign exchange. Such controls rapidly evolved into an explicit strategy to promote import-substituting industrialization behind high and variable import protection, which was backed by central planning to allocate resources. A self-interested bureaucracy, famously dubbed the "license raj" by Bhagwati and Desai (1970), implemented a plethora of controls and restrictions on private sector expansion and exporting. A strict and cumbersome system of licensing and quotas was applied to imports of capital goods, consumer goods, and other inputs. To this formidable battery of trade and investment controls were added policies to foster indigenous technology. Controls were applied at various stages to access foreign technology in the form of FDI and licensing agreements. For instance, under the Foreign Exchange Regulations Act of 1973, foreign ownership beyond 40 percent equity was usually not permitted. For licensing, the government imposed strict controls on payments permitted and life of the contract. Shielded from competition, a handful of large private firms and state-owned enterprises occupied monopoly positions in major industrial and service sectors. Interestingly, in the late 1970s, India's manufacturing sector was smaller than China's. India's manufacturing sector made up 17 percent of GDP in 1978, compared with 41 percent in China.

There were attempts at partial liberalization of imports and exports in phase two. For instance, in 1979, India introduced an open general licensing list that permitted limited imports of machinery and raw materials not produced domestically. In the mid-1980s, a few measures to promote exports were undertaken, including a passbook scheme for duty-free imports for exporters and the setting of the exchange rate at a more realistic level. Partial liberalization contributed to India's export development in the second half of the 1980s. Albeit from a low base, India's exports of goods and services rose modestly from $8.6 billion to $12.2 billion between 1978 and 1985. India's share of world exports of goods and services, however, fell from 0.6 percent to 0.5

percent during the same period. The hallmark of the trade and investment regime during phases one and two was an anti-export bias that held back export growth and diversification. Tight controls on technology imports meant that there was only a trickle of FDI inflows, and few technology licenses were granted. Overprotection resulted in technological obsolescence, and Indian industry rapidly fell behind world technology frontiers (Lall 1987).[5] Largely shut out from external markets and technology transfer, India's economy grew unremarkably at the so-called Hindu rate of 3.5 percent per year during the period 1950–1980.

> *Overprotection resulted in technological obsolescence, and Indian industry fell behind*

Trade and Investment Reforms

In phase three, reforms of India's import-substituting industrializing strategy were undertaken from the 1990s onward. A package of trade and investment reforms were introduced in 1991 and followed by deeper reforms over time, leading to four key changes as follows.

First, in a sweeping liberalization on the trade front, import licensing on machinery and raw materials was abolished in 1991. Licensing on consumer goods was abolished in 2001. This meant that import tariffs became the main protective instrument after 1991.

Second, a gradual reduction in the dispersion of high and variable import tariffs, which had risen significantly in the 1980s, also began in 1991. Tariff reform focused on a gradual compression of the top tariff rates, with simultaneous rationalization of the tariff structure via a reduction in the number of tariff bands.

Third, a depreciated exchange rate was maintained to boost export competitiveness, and better access to foreign exchange for exporting was introduced. The dual exchange rate was unified and current account convertibility commenced in 1994, in line with International Monetary Fund (IMF) Article VII obligations.

Fourth, a formal FDI policy was adopted in 1996 and restrictions on foreign ownership were gradually liberalized. A system of automatic clearance for FDI proposals fulfilling various conditions (e.g., ownership levels of 50 percent, 51 percent, 74 percent, and 100 percent) and new sectors (e.g., mining, banking, software, telecommunications, and various services) were opened up to foreign ownership. Subsequently, 100 percent foreign ownership was permitted in manufacturing with some exceptions, such as defense-related sectors, cigarettes, and items reserved for the small-scale industrial sector. In 2005, a Special Economic Zones Act was passed to promote exports from both foreign and local enterprises more systematically. These zones offered various fiscal and financial incentives to decentralize FDI into different regions in India.

The post-1991 reforms had a significant impact on India's profile as an international investment destination. Between 1978–1990 and 1991–2010, average annual FDI inflows increased from a tiny $100 million to an unprecedented $9.5 billion (table 8). The annual averages mask the fact that most of the increase in FDI inflows took place in the second decade after the 1991 reforms, indicating a notable lag between the enactment of policy reforms and major FDI inflows. Annual average FDI inflows rose multifold from $2.5 billion to $20 billion between 1991–2002 and 2003–2010.

> *Post-1991 reforms radically impacted India's profile as an international investment destination*

FDI inflows peaked at $41.6 billion in 2008. But the global financial crisis exerted a significant negative effect on inward investment into India, and FDI inflows fell from this peak level to $34.6 billion in 2009 and remained depressed at $21 billion in 2010. Cumulative FDI inflows amounted to $191.3 billion in 1978–2010, with $155.3 billion occurring in the 1991–2010 period.

Following a focus on domestic manufacturing, FDI flows have increasingly shifted toward services, particularly information and communications technology (ICT) services and financial services. The United States is the single largest source of FDI into India after Mauritius, making up about 16 percent of total FDI inflows during 1991–2006 (Kumar and Sharma 2009, 39). East Asian economies account for another 14 percent and EU countries comprise 24 percent.

The attraction of significant FDI inflows into India is a major achievement of the 1991 reforms. The post-2003 surge in FDI flows is particularly encouraging, and the figures for 2008 and 2009 are starting to match FDI inflows into China in the 1990s. Nonetheless, cumulative FDI inflows are below the levels experienced by China and other high-performing East Asian economies. For instance, cumulative FDI inflows into India during 1978–2010 are only one-sixth of China's for the same period. The entry of FDI into India brought new technologies, skills, and marketing connections, and began the process of making Indian manufacturing more internationally competitive. Thus far, India has yet to emulate East Asia's example of fully exploiting the potential for export-oriented FDI inflows into manufacturing. Foreign direct investment into Indian manufacturing has largely focused on serving the large domestic market rather than exports. It is estimated that the share of multinational enterprises in India's exports is small, at less than 10 percent, compared with 54 percent in China (Kumar and Sharma 2009, 37; Government of the People's Republic of China-Ministry of Commerce 2011).

> ## FDI into Indian manufacturing is focused on the large domestic market rather than exports

The smaller FDI inflows relative to China and an orientation toward the domestic market in the first decade of Indian reforms may be due to two factors. First, the incremental and somewhat cumbersome process of liberalizing FDI rules led to some criticism that India's FDI regulations in the first reform decade were complicated and opaque. Furthermore, inspite of some progress, many areas of Indian economic activity remain closed to FDI including nuclear, multi-brand retail, lottery and betting, foreign airlines, much of agriculture, and parts of small-scale industry. Second, the large domestic market (with a growing base of middle class consumers hungry for overseas products) acted as a magnet for the entry of domestic market-oriented FDI following the 1991 reforms.

Another aspect of India's post-1991 reforms is the emergence of outward investment. India had limited outward investment in the first decade-and-a-half of reform, but has seen a marked increase thereafter. India's annual average outward FDI increased from a relatively small base of $1 billion to $16.7 billion between 1995–2005 and 2006–2008 (table 8). However, there was a fall in outward investment to $14.9 billion in 2009 as a result of the global financial crisis. India's cumulative outward investment amounted to $73.1 billion in 1995–2009, which is equivalent to about 40 percent of China's during the same period.

Research suggests three interesting features of Indian foreign acquisitions during 2000–2006 (see Athukorala 2009). First, most Indian overseas investors are part of large business conglomerates, with as few as 15 firms accounting for over 80 percent of the value of overseas acquisitions. Second, Indian overseas investment is concentrated in a handful of sectors. The main sectors in terms of the total value of Indian foreign acquisitions were: information technology (24.3 percent), pharmaceuticals (16.3 percent), petroleum and natural gas (15 percent), consumer goods (13.4 percent), and steel (11.2 percent). Third, about 80 percent of total Indian acquisitions were in developed countries, particularly the United States and the United Kingdom.

Import Liberalization and Exchange Rates
Import tariffs, which became the main protective instrument following the abolition of licensing, steadily fell during the post-1991 period. On the eve of the 1991 reforms, India was reputed to have the highest import tariffs in the developing world, along with a significant dispersion of import tariffs. In 1991, the simple average of all tariffs was 113 percent, with the highest tariff rate at 355 percent (Panagariya 2004, 7). A reduction occurred thereafter, with simple average tariffs falling from this peak to 38.7 percent in 1996, and still further to 12.9 percent in 2009 (see table 9). The main thrust of tariff reduction since 1991 has been on nonagricultural products rather than agricultural products. Tariffs on nonagricultural products fell somewhat modestly from 40.1 percent to 31.4 percent between 1996

> *Despite significant reductions, India's average import tariffs remain higher than China's*

and 2001, but the pace of tariff reduction accelerated in recent years, with such tariffs falling to historic lows of 10.1 percent in 2008. In contrast, tariffs on primary products actually rose from 23.1 percent to 36.3 percent between 1996 and 2001, and subsequently fell slightly to 31.8 percent in 2009. In spite of progress in tariff reduction, India's average import tariffs remain higher than China's. While a narrow gap exists on the average rates for nonagricultural tariffs, India's average import tariffs on agricultural products are double those of China's.

The growing gap between agricultural and nonagricultural tariffs in India also raised the dispersion in tariffs. As table 10 shows, there is significant dispersion in the tariffs for nonagricultural products, which range from 7.2 percent for electrical machinery to 29.8 percent for fish and fish products. The dispersion of tariffs is considerably higher, however, for agricultural products, ranging from 12 percent for cotton to 70.8 percent for beverages and tobacco. Accordingly, tariff dispersion seems higher in India than in China.

Unification of the dual exchange rate, along with current account convertibility, increased the potency of the exchange rate as a trade policy instrument and improved foreign exchange availability for exporters. As figure 2 shows, India maintained a stable and predictable REER between January 2000 and May 2005. Since mid-2005, however, the REER has tended to behave more erratically, with short periods of sharp depreciation followed by sharp appreciation. More volatile REER behavior since 2005 reflects differences in inflation between India and its major trading partners. Particularly worrisome is the emergence of an appreciating trend after March 2009 linked to rising inflation in India. Rising commodity and fuel prices are among the main causes of rising inflation. Accordingly, the REER supported exporting activity between 2000 and mid-2005, but has provided more mixed signals in recent years.

Comparing Reforms and Export Outcomes

China and India have each pursued distinctive styles of reforms as they shifted to outward-oriented, market-based economies after long periods of inward-oriented, centrally planned policies. Contrary to the prevailing orthodoxy that emphasized the merits of "big bang," comprehensive reforms such as those pursued by Russia, the giants initiated gradual and incremental reforms over several decades, starting in the late-1970s. The giants' gradualist approach reflects concerns about the strength of the private

The giants rejected Russian-style 'big bang' reforms in favor of gradual and incremental reforms

sector supply response to reforms, the long process of creating market institutions, and the social consequences of economic adjustment. China and India differ, however, in their processes of implementing a gradual approach to reforms, which include timing, speed, stages, and specific measures adopted. Accordingly, differences in trade and investment policies have influenced China's rise as a massive global exporter of manufactures and India's expansion into high-skill service exports alongside manufactures.

China was swifter, more coordinated, and more credible in its overall reform process than India. It introduced an open door to FDI in 1978, while India's major reforms came as late as 1991. Attracting export-oriented FDI into the manufacturing sector became the cornerstone of China's trade and investment policies in the early years of reform, and it underlies China's success in manufactured exports. China evolved a comprehensive FDI policy that enabled it to attract record inflows of export-oriented FDI into manufacturing and to technologically upgrade it over time (via joint ventures and technology transfer). This comprehensive FDI policy included the deregulation of entry rules, as well as the introduction of active policies such as incentives, infrastructure, and technology support. Another FDI spillover is the growth of Chinese outward investment to Asia and the rest of the world. Over time, Chinese outward investment is expected to become a major driver of global FDI in manufacturing industries, as large Chinese firms seek new market opportunities.

India was slower in adopting a comprehensive policy framework for export-oriented FDI. It initially focused on liberalizing restrictions on foreign ownership, which is perhaps insufficient in a highly competitive international environment for attracting export-oriented FDI. For instance, other measures like SEZ legislation only date to 2005. Moreover, the somewhat cumbersome process of reforming FDI rules led to criticisms by foreign investors that the country's FDI regime was complicated and non-transparent. FDI inflows increased but remained below expected levels in the first decade after the reforms indicating caution about foreign investment in the Indian economy. Nonetheless, an improvement in India's investment climate in the second reform decade was accompanied by a surge in FDI inflows, particularly into services. If the FDI surge continues, India has the potential to become a significant global services hub with a respectable manufacturing export base.

Export promotion via FDI took place in China alongside controlled liberalization of a protected domestic sector. China was cautious in reforming its import control regime during the early transition years, but the process was strengthened from 1992 onwards by reforms to accede to the WTO. Steady progress in tariff reform occurred, so that China has presently emerged as one of the more open economies in the developing world. Increased import competition induced increased efficiency, industrial restructuring, and exporting in a formerly protected domestic enterprise sector. India dramatically abolished import licensing on machinery and raw materials in 1991, and tariff reform has resulted in a far more open import regime than ever before. Nonetheless, India's average tariffs and their dispersion still remain higher than China's.

In an environment of gradual tariff reform, exchange rate management became a critical tool to encourage exporting activity in the giants. China introduced currency convertibility on current account transactions, while India unified the dual exchange rate and commenced current account convertibility. Following improved access to foreign exchange, the giants both pursued managed floating exchange rate policies to maintain relatively stable and predictable nominal exchange rates. Both also had some success in maintaining a favorable REER for exporting activity during the 2000s, but China seems to have done somewhat better than India in this regard.

5. Regionalism and FTAs

This section considers the question of whether the giants' recent emphasis on FTAs is detrimental to exports. In another marked shift in trade and investment regimes since the early 2000s, the giants have each pursued bilateral and regional trade agreements alongside multilateralism. These moves have promoted some concerns about the possible detrimental impact of FTAs on exporting for two reasons. One is the shallow coverage of FTAs, which are said to be quite liberalizing when it comes to the trade of goods, with the exception of agriculture, but quite thin and vague in scope compared with most agreements formed in the Americas or across the Pacific (Suominen 2009). Second, there is the problem of the so-called Asian "noodle bowl" of FTAs. Informed by Jagdish Bhagwati's famous insight of a spaghetti bowl of FTAs and applied to Asia, the noodle bowl description suggests that different tariffs and rules of origin in multiple FTAs have resulted in the problem of criss-crossing agreements, which are characterized by excessive exclusions and special treatment (Baldwin 2008). Quite apart from a potential distortion of trade toward bilateral channels, it is suggested that firms face large administrative burdens, such as the need to deal with multiple rules of origin, which results in the FTAs being little used. Are these concerns valid?

> *The complex Asian 'noodle bowl' of foreign trade agreements may cause problems*

Rationale for FTAs

By June 2011, the giants were among the region's leaders in FTA activity, with 11 FTAs in effect in both China and India (table 11). The number of FTAs under negotiation and FTAs proposed suggests that such activity will rise in the future, as China has another 13 agreements in the pipeline and India another 20. Meanwhile, a relatively limited (goods only) Asia-Pacific Trade Agreement (APTA) is the only FTA between China and India.

The giants' interest in FTAs may seem somewhat surprising. While India is a founding WTO member, China only joined the WTO in 2001. This interest can be attributed to three main causes:[6] (1) the expansion of European and North American FTA-led regionalism, which highlights large economic gains (e.g., economies of scale, specialization, and inward investment) available from integrating fragmented regional markets; (2) the lack of progress in the multilateral WTO Doha Round trade negotiations, which has encouraged FTAs to be considered as an alternative means of securing market access for goods and services, as well as venturing into new trade issues not covered by the Doha Round; and (3) increasing recognition that FTAs are part of a supporting policy framework for deepening production networks and supply chains formed by global multinational corporations (MNCs) and emerging Asian firms.

Reflecting its relatively recent FTA experience, China has FTAs with trading partners in the near vicinity and developing world—

Table 11. Classification of China and India FTAs in Effect (as of June 2011)

Country	FTA	Goods liberalization[a]	Coverage of services sectors[b]	Coverage of Singapore Issues[c]
CHINA				
1	Asia-Pacific Trade Agreement (2001)	partial	no provision	no provision
2	PRC-Thailand FTA (2003)	partial	no provision	no provision
3	PRC-Hong Kong CEPA (2004)	WTO-compliant	partial	no provision
4	PRC-Macao CEPA (2004)	WTO-compliant	partial	no provision
5	ASEAN-China FTA (2005)	WTO-compliant	partial	partial (investment)
6	PRC-Chile FTA (2006)	WTO-compliant	partial	partial (trade facilitation)
7	New Zealand-China FTA (2008)	WTO-compliant	partial	partial (investment, trade facilitation)
8	PRC-Pakistan FTA (2007)	partial	partial	partial (investment)
9	PRC-Singapore FTA (2008)	WTO-compliant	comprehensive	partial (trade facilitation)
10	PRC-Peru FTA (2009)	WTO-compliant	partial	partial (investment, trade facilitation)
11	Cross-Strait Economic Cooperation Framework Agreement (2010)[d]	partial	partial	partial (investment)
INDIA				
1	Asia-Pacific Trade Agreement (1976)	partial	no provision	no provision
2	India-Sri Lanka FTA (2001)	WTO-compliant	no provision	no provision
3	Indo-Nepal Treaty of Trade (2002)	partial	no provision	partial (trade facilitation)
4	India-Afghanistan PTA[e] (2003)	partial	no provision	no provision
5	India-Singapore CECA (2005)	WTO-compliant	comprehensive	partial (investment, trade facilitation)
6	South Asian FTA (2006)	partial	partial (SATIS signed)[f]	partial (trade facilitation)
7	India-Bhutan Trade Agreement (2006)	partial	no provision	partial (trade facilitation)
8	India-Chile PTA (2007)	partial	no provision	no provision

Table 11. Classification of China and India FTAs in Effect (as of June 2011) (continued)

Country	FTA	Goods liberalization[a]	Coverage of services sectors[b]	Coverage of Singapore Issues[c]
INDIA				
9	India-MERCOSUR PTA (2009)	partial	no provision	no provision
10	India-Korea CEPA (2009)	WTO-compliant	comprehensive	comprehensive (government procurement cooperation only)
11	ASEAN-India FTA (2009)	partial	no provision	partial (customs procedure cooperation only)

Source: Author's estimates based on ADB, Asia Regional Integration Center, http://aric.adb.org, accessed June 2011.
Notes:
[a]An FTA is "WTO-compliant" following GATT Article 24, where tariffs are eliminated on at least 85 percent of either or both FTA members' tariff lines (or goods traded) within 10 years. Otherwise, it has partial coverage.
[b]Comprehensive coverage if an FTA covers the 5 key sectors of the GATS—business and professional services, communications services, financial services, transport services, and labor mobility/entry of businesspersons. No provision means there is no liberalization provision on services sector. Partial are those not otherwise classified as comprehensive or no provision.
[c]Comprehensive are those that cover all the Singapore issues of investment, competition policy, government procurement, and trade facilitation. Partial if only 1 to 3 Singapore issues are in the FTAs. No provision means those without any provision on Singapore issues.
[d]This refers to the FTA between China and Taipei that came into effect on September 12, 2010.
[e]PTA refers to preferential trade agreement.
[f]SATIS stands for SAARC Agreement on Trade in Services. SAARC stands for South Asian Association for Regional Cooperation.

ASEAN members, Hong Kong, Taipei, Macao, Pakistan, Chile, and Peru—but only one agreement with a developed economy, New Zealand. China's FTA strategy appears driven by economic motivations related to its emergence as the global factory and to its pivotal role in Asian production networks. China views FTAs as supporting the functioning of Asian production networks in electronics and automotives, and as a means of gaining preferential market access for manufactured exports. To this end, the ASEAN-China FTA, which is an important building block for an Asia-wide FTA, has effectively created the

China's FTA strategy is linked to its emergence as the global factory

world's largest free trade zone and facilitated the parts-and-components trade in ASEAN economies and final assembly in China. The agreements with Hong Kong, Taipei, and Macao are natural extensions of the free trade zone into the region. The impetus for such agreements to reduce trade barriers and costs has come from overseas Chinese investors who account for the bulk of inward investment into China. The FTA with Pakistan provides initial access to the large and growing South Asian market. The FTA with New Zealand provides China with an opportunity to learn about negotiating comprehensive, next-generation FTAs with developed countries, as well as to attract FDI and technology transfers in the dairy industry. The FTAs with Chile and Peru are entry points into the Latin American market and a means of fostering closer transpacific cooperation.

China's future FTAs consist of a mix of subregional and bilateral agreements. Prominent among the subregional FTAs is a China–Japan–South Korea agreement, which is critical to the formation of an Asia-wide FTA and the deepening of production networks. FTAs with the South African Customs Union and Gulf Cooperation Council facilitate access to commodity imports for fueling China's rapid industrialization and to regional markets for its manufactured exports. Unlike in India, there is little sign of FTA discussions with China's major trading partners in the developed world—notably the European Union (EU) and the United States—which may reflect the trading partners' concerns about the impact of China's highly competitive manufactured exports on domestic employment. For the same reason, there has been little movement in official FTA discussions with India.

China seems to be experimenting with alternative formats for FTAs in an attempt to eventually evolve a template akin to what the United States uses for FTA negotiations. In earlier FTAs with ASEAN and Chile, China followed a gradual approach, whereby goods were liberalized first, then services and investment. A simultaneous approach, however, characterizes more recent bilateral FTAs with New Zealand and Singapore.

With a smaller manufacturing base and the relatively late adoption of trade liberalization, India's initial motivation for concluding FTAs appears to have been different from China's. Motivated by a political commitment to the Non-Aligned Movement, India has long supported the expansion of South-South trade though agreements focused on market access for goods trading. In this vein, it was party to the region's first agreement (the Asia-Pacific Trade Agreement) as early as 1976. Following a long period of detailed negotiation, a spate of bilateral FTAs were enacted with smaller South Asian neighbors, including Afghanistan, Bhutan, Nepal, and Sri Lanka; a subregional South Asian Free Trade Area was opened in an attempt to

India's FTAs reflected its political commitments to the Non-Aligned Movement

access markets in Bangladesh and Pakistan; and bilateral agreements with Chile and Mercosur were reached. The South-South thrust of India's FTA strategy continues, and agreements are under negotiation with several Latin American and African countries. India's FTA strategy evolved to encompass major trading partners, and market access became more prominent after the 1991 economic reforms.

Recent extensions reflect its Look East Policy of fostering economic ties with economically important East Asia, as well as efforts to accommodate its growing services sector's access to developed countries. India has put into effect FTAs with ASEAN, Singapore, and South Korea as stepping-stones toward an ASEAN+6 FTA. More recently, in early 2011, India signed FTAs with Japan and Malaysia. It is also engaged in active FTA negotiations with several developed countries, including the EU, Australia, New Zealand, Canada, and the four members of the European Free Trade Association (EFTA).[7] The expressed interested of developed countries in negotiating FTAs with India reflects complementarities in factor endowments and trade patterns, as well as a recent surge in multinational investment focused on the large domestic Indian market.

Quality of FTAs

What is the quality of China's and India's existing FTAs in relation to best practices? Evaluating FTA quality against best practices is difficult for two reasons. First, it requires detailed and often painstaking examination of the legal texts of FTAs. Second, an internationally accepted methodology for assessing the quality of FTA provisions against best practices is absent. One way forward is to attempt to evaluate the compatibility of China's and India's FTAs against existing (or future) global rules. Building on recent research, some simple legal and economic evaluation criteria were developed to gauge the giants' FTAs according to tariff elimination on the goods trade, coverage of services sectors, and coverage of trade issues beyond goods and services (Plummer 2007; Wignaraja and Lazaro 2010). The tariff elimination criteria reflected Article 24 of the General Agreement on Tariffs and Trade (GATT). FTAs that eliminated tariffs on at least 85 percent of tariff lines (of either or all FTA partners) within 10 years were classed as WTO-compliant. The criteria for services liberalization relied on the coverage of sectors included in the General Agreement on Trade in Services (GATS). FTAs that covered five key sectors of the GATS were considered "comprehensive." Those with less than five sectors were categorized as "partial," and those without any coverage as "no provision." The four so-called Singapore issues in the context of WTO negotiations—investment, competition policy, government procurement, and trade facilitation—are convenient for examining trade issues beyond goods and services. The Singapore issues refer to four working groups set up during the WTO Ministerial Conference of 1996 in Singapore. These groups are tasked with four key issues: (1) transparency in government procurement, (2) trade facilitation (customs issues), (3) trade and investment, and (4) trade and competition. The four Singapore issues were conditionally included in the work program for the Doha Development Round global trade talks, but were dropped at the WTO Ministerial Conference in Cancún in 2004. FTAs that covered all four Singapore issues were classed as comprehensive, and the remainder as partial or no provision.

Table 11 presents the details of the classification system and the results for individual FTAs in China and India. Legal texts from the Asian Development Bank (ADB)'s FTA database were used for the empirical application of these criteria. The results are quite revealing about the quality of China's and India's FTAs in terms of existing or future global rules. The key findings are given below.

The overall quality of China's and India's trade agreements varies. Of the giants' 22 FTAs in effect, 10 are WTO-compliant on goods liberalization, three are comprehensive in services coverage, and one is comprehensive in coverage of Singapore issues. The best FTAs are probably the China-Singapore FTA, which is WTO-compliant on goods and comprehensive in services coverage, and the India-Korea Comprehensive Economic Partnership Agreement (CEPA), which is comprehensive in both services coverage and Singapore issues, in addition to being WTO-compliant on goods.

In terms of goods liberalization, China's FTAs seem better than India's. Seven of China's FTAs are WTO-compliant, compared with three for India. Some examples of WTO-compliant agreements are useful to highlight differences in the giants' approaches with their trading partners. Under the China-Singapore FTA, 95 percent of China's tariff lines are eliminated within one year. Singapore, of course, has virtually zero

> *In terms of goods liberalization, China's FTAs seem better than India's*

tariffs for most items, and tariff elimination is not considered a major trade policy issue. The New Zealand-China FTA allows for immediate elimination of 35 percent of China's tariff lines upon entry into force (i.e., when the agreement became legally binding on 1 October 2008) and 96 percent within eight years. The ASEAN-China FTA allows for longer adjustment periods for least developed countries (LDCs) and, accordingly, eliminates 90 percent of the tariff lines of China and the ASEAN-6 economies within five years, while the economies of Cambodia, Myanmar, Laos, and Vietnam have 10 years. Meanwhile, the India-Korea FTA liberalizes 75 percent of India's tariff lines within eight years and 93 percent of South Korea's. The India-Singapore FTA immediately eliminates tariffs on 80 percent of the value of India's imports from Singapore.

The coverage of services also seems better in China's FTAs than in India's. The China-Singapore FTA allows for comprehensive coverage of services, while another seven of China's FTAs cover partial liberalization in services. The China-Singapore agreement significantly builds on the ASEAN-China FTA by allowing for the movement of "natural persons." Otherwise known as "Mode 4," this covers the international supply of services through the movement of service suppliers (e.g., independent professionals) or those who work for a service supplier. By comparison, and with the notable exceptions of the India–South Korea Comprehensive Economic Partnership Agreement

(CEPA) and the India-Singapore Comprehensive Economic Cooperation Agreement (CECA), India's FTAs seem more limited in services coverage. In a move to extend services coverage to the regional level, a South Asian Trade in Services Agreement was signed in April 2010.

The four Singapore issues are selectively covered in the giants' FTAs. Seven of China's FTAs cover one or two Singapore issues. For instance, investment and trade facilitation[8] are both covered in the China–New Zealand FTA and the China-Peru FTA, while the China-Pakistan FTA and the Economic Cooperation Framework Agreement (ECFA) cover only investment. More sensitive issues of government procurement and competition policy are absent from China's FTAs. Meanwhile, the India–South Korea FTA comprehensively covers three Singapore issues. While there is no separate chapter on government procurement, there is a cooperation provision on government procurement that opens the door for liberalization in this difficult area. Another four of India's FTAs, including the South Asia Free Trade Area (SAFTA), only cover trade facilitation, while the India-Singapore FTA covers both trade facilitation and investment. China's and India's remaining FTAs exclude the Singapore issues altogether.

Business Use of FTAs

Unfortunately, neither China nor India publishes official data on FTA use from certificates of origin or information on impediments to using FTAs. This is a major gap that needs to be addressed in the future. Nonetheless, it is possible to explore this issue by looking at trade with FTA partners, which is indicative of potential use, and by examining evidence from firm surveys.

The number of FTAs is relatively easy to track over time, but by themselves the numbers do not indicate the importance of FTAs to economic activity or trade at the national level. It is informative to get an idea of how much of a country's world trade is covered by FTA provisions. This is difficult to measure because of exceptions and exclusions contained in many agreements. Furthermore, official statistics on utilization rates of FTA preferences in Asia are hard to come by, and published data on the direction of services trade do not exist. Nevertheless, by making the bold assumption that all goods trade is covered by concluded FTAs, indicative estimates can be obtained. The

Table 12. Chinese Firms' Utilization of FTA Preferences and Impediments to Use

	% respondents
1. FTA utilization rate	45.0
2. Impediments to using FTAs[a]	
Lack of information	45.1
Use of EPZ schemes or ITA	8.8
Delays and administrative costs	10.6
Small preference margins	14.2
Too many exclusions	4.4
Rent seeking	5.3
NTM in FTA partners	6.2
Confidentiality of information required	10.6
Number of respondents	226

Source: Zhang (2011). Data collected in 2008.
Notes: Based on survey results.
[a]Multiple responses were allowed.

giants' increasing FTA numbers have been accompanied by the growing importance of trade with FTA partners over the first decade of the 2000s. While the majority of international trade is still with non-FTA partners, an estimate was made that about 27 percent of China's total trade and 23 percent of India's was potentially covered by FTAs in 2008.[9] Encouragingly, these figures are up considerably, from less than 5 percent in 2003.

Table 12 provides recent data on the use of FTAs in Chinese firms, as well as impediments to FTA use. These are from Zhang (2011) and were collected in 2008 as a part of a multicountry, multienterprise survey conducted by the Asian Development Bank and various partners. FTA use in China is higher than previously thought, and much higher than elsewhere in Asia (Baldwin 2008). About 45 percent of the firms in the countrywide Chinese survey said that they had used FTAs, and more said they planned to do so in the future (Zhang 2011). This compares with 29 percent for Japanese firms, 25 percent for Thai firms, 21 percent for South Korean firms, 20 percent for Singaporean firms, and 20 percent for firms in the Philippines (see Kawai and Wignaraja, eds. 2011). Use of FTAs in China is closely linked to innovation and learning processes at the firm level, thereby underlining the importance of technology-based approaches to trade. Econometric analysis of the decision to export among a sample of Chinese firms reveals that FTA use, export experience, foreign owner-ship, and R&D expenditures all influence the probability of exporting (Wignaraja 2010).

Zhang (2011) also highlights impediments to using FTAs at the firm level in China (see table 12). Interestingly, few firms seemed concerned by the Asian noodle bowl effect, with only 6 percent of the Chinese sample expressing concerns about significant transaction costs arising from multiple rules of origin in overlapping agreements. As more FTAs come into effect, however, the noodle bowl remains a future risk for the region. As of 2011, however, the key impediments to FTA use in China turned out to be a lack of information on FTA provisions and business impacts, nontariff measures in overseas mar-kets, small margins of preference, and the availability of alternative export incentives (e.g., export processing zone schemes and the Infor-mation Technology Agreement).

Unfortunately, information on use of FTAs is not yet available for Indian firms from either the Asian Development Bank survey or other sources. But discussions with the Federation of Indian Cham-bers of Commerce and Industry (FICCI) suggested that its members were increasingly aware of the benefits of FTAs, such as the Indo-Lanka FTA and the ASEAN-India FTA, and they had begun to use them to facilitate the goods and services trade with FTA partners.[10] They also said that India's FTAs with Sri Lanka and ASEAN had facilitated an increase in intraregional investment in manufacturing and IT services.

Thus, there seems little evidence of detrimental effects on exports of China's and India's FTAs. The giants' FTA strategies still appear to be in the formative stages. China's FTAs with regional developing economies are geared towards supporting its role as the global factory and the deepening its production networks. From an initial focus on

South-South trade, India has recently moved towards seeking market access to East Asia and major developed countries. China's FTAs seem to have better coverage in terms of goods and services. FTA use at least in China also seems higher than expected. Nonetheless, both countries can improve the coverage of Singapore issues in future FTAs and adopt best practices in designing rules of origin and origin administration. The issue of how to improve business use of FTAs is examined further in Section 6.

> *FTA use in China is higher than expected, and much higher than elsewhere in Asia*

6. Challenges for Sustaining Trade-led Growth

Evolving World Economic Scenario

Growth in China and India has rebounded from the global financial crisis, while the world economy remains sluggish (Asian Development Bank, 2011a). The global financial crisis marked the end of a period of respectable world growth and expanding employment in major industrial economies. Unprecedented fiscal stimulus efforts coupled with low interest rates averted a 1930s-style economic depression. Nonetheless, slow economic growth with high unemployment in much of the developed world appears to characterize the likely scenario in the medium term.[11] This somewhat pessimistic scenario is linked to unusually high levels of public debt, the crisis in the eurozone economies, lackluster private investment, and fragile consumer confidence. Some developed countries are in the process of making large cuts in public expenditures, which may accentuate the slowdown, at least in the short run. A lack of progress on the WTO Doha Round concerning the magnitude of reductions in agricultural subsidies and industrial tariffs continues to deprive the world economy of a major source of trade-led growth. Added to this are risks to world growth associated with soft labor and housing markets in the United States, vulnerable sovereign debt positions in the eurozone, the aftermath of the disasters in Japan, and rising commodity prices (Asian Development Bank, 2011a). Developing Asia, including China and India, have provided much-needed support to the world economy during the downturn and recovery, but it is unclear how far the region can extend this role without a stronger recovery in the developed world. While the magnitude of world economic growth in the medium term is difficult to forecast, the consensus forecast points in a downward direction. Without strong demand from developed markets, the two giants will increasingly have to rely on inter-Asian demand and South-South cooperation for continued growth and exports.

Emerging literature suggests that the continued rise of the giants in the world economy will be shaped by several important economic policy challenges. These include demographics, agricultural reform, financial integration, the environment, and governance (see, for instance, Winters and Yusuf 2007; Bardhan 2010; Gerhaeusser et al. 2010). In addition to these, seven specific policy challenges are likely to impact upon trade-led growth of the giants in the post–global financial crisis world economy: (1) entering production networks, (2) promoting industrial technology development, (3) investing in infrastructure and reducing red tape, (4) increasing FTA use by businesses, (5) managing exchange rates, (6) mitigating the risk of protectionism, and (7) reducing poverty. How well the giants tackle these challenges will partly determine the continued pace of their trade-led growth in the medium term.

Entering Production Networks

Major trends in China's and India's trade performance were discussed in Section 2, including China's relatively impressive success in producing for world markets and the rise in technological sophistication of its exports, which is more typical of a highly developed country. It has been argued that this conclusion did not factor in the large amount of processing trade in sectors that may be termed high technology. Accordingly, the rise in technological sophistication in China's exports could be "nothing but a statistical mirage due to processing trade" (Feenstra and Wei 2010, 8). Distinguishing between ordinary versus processing trade in China's total exports[12] suggests that the proportion of processing trade in total exports rose from 47 percent in 1992 to a peak of 57 percent in 1999, and then fell to 53 percent in 2006 (Feenstra and Wei 2010). A similar pattern is visible on the import side.

Processing trade in China can be traced to the spread of Asia's advanced production networks, which have propelled Asia's rise as the global factory over several decades (Borrus, Ernst, and Haggard 2000; Asian Development Bank 2011b). Production processes have been broken into smaller processes, with each process located in the most cost-effective economy, further improving efficiency. Through strategies of innovation and learning, Asian firms acquired the requisite technological capabilities to either compete internationally or become suppliers to multinational corporations (MNCs) (Mathews and Cho 2000; Wignaraja 2011). This involved developing production engineering skills to use imported technologies efficiently and successfully plugging into the advanced global production networks formed by MNCs and local suppliers. As systematic innovation and learning took place at the firm level, a shift from labor-intensive exports (e.g., textiles, garments, and footwear) to more technology-intensive exports (e.g., chemicals, ships, electric appliances, electronics, and automobiles) occurred in Asia. Several factors (including falling trade barriers and logistic costs, technological progress, and rising factor costs at core production locations) have spurred the decentralization of production networks to the most cost-effective locations. Trade within Asia increased significantly from 37 percent of total trade to 56 percent between 1980 and 2008, led by trade in parts and components (Kawai and Wignaraja 2011). This trend seems set to continue with further regional liberalization via FTAs (Petri 2008).

China and India seem to face different challenges relating to global production networks. With an abundance of cheap and skilled labor, modern infrastructure, and a relatively business-friendly environment, China has become Asia's cost-effective magnet for the assembly of final goods. Amidst rising real wages and other factor costs, the future challenge for China is how to sustain its position as a cost-effective production location and increase domestic value added. India is an important participant in global services value chains (e.g., information

China is a magnet for its cheap, skilled labor; modern infrastructure; and business-friendly environment

technology and business process outsourcing) and has also begun to enter production networks in some manufacturing sectors (e.g., steel and automotives). India's challenge is how to consolidate its role as a cost-effective production center and attract inward investment in processing trade. Important measures to facilitate the giants' closer integration into production networks include continuing to attract export-oriented FDI, promoting industrial technology development, investing in infrastructure, and reducing bureaucratic procedures to doing business and increasing FTA use.

Promoting Industrial Technology Development

For China and India, entering production networks and shifting into new areas of comparative advantage require dedicated promotion of industrial technology development, along with continuing gradual liberalization of trade and investment regimes (Lall 2001; Borrus, Ernst, and Haggard 2000; Wignaraja 2003). Technology transfer from abroad through FDI is most effective when combined with domestic technological efforts to absorb imported technologies efficiently. Domestic technological efforts (including R&D) take place within a national innovation system characterized by interactions between firms and institutions.

R&D effort is a vital prerequisite for maintaining competitiveness in medium- and high-technology industries, and ensuring technology spillovers from FDI to local firms. How do the giants fare? Table 13 shows two measures of R&D efforts in China and India since 1996:

> *By 2007, China had nearly eight times as many R&D people as India*

R&D expenditures as a percentage of GDP and the number of researchers in R&D per million people. The data indicate India lags significantly behind China in both measures. In 1996, China (0.6 percent) and India (0.7 percent) spent about the same on R&D as a percentage of GDP. By 2007, China's R&D had more than doubled to 1.5 percent, while India's stagnated at 0.8 percent. A much larger technology gap is visible in terms of researchers in R&D per million people. In 1996, China had nearly three times as many researchers in R&D as India. By 2007, China had nearly eight times as many researchers as India.

Industrial R&D and the national innovation systems in the giants are important priorities for further development. Studies have highlighted future challenges in this regard. According to Dahlman and

Table 13. Infrastructure, Business Regulation, and Technology, Most Recent Estimates

Indicators	Year	CHINA	INDIA
Infrastructure spending (% of GDP)[a]	2008	11	6
Quality of overall infrastructure[b]	2010–2011	72	91
Quality of roads[b]	2010–2011	53	90
Quality of electricity supply[b]	2010–2011	52	110
Ease of doing business index (1=most business-friendly regulations)[c]	2010	79	134
Starting a business[c]	2010	151	165
Registering property[c]	2010	38	94
Enforcing contracts[c]	2010	15	182
Closing a business[c]	2010	68	134
Research and development expenditure (% of GDP)[d]	1996	0.6	0.7
	2007	1.5	0.8
Researchers in R&D (per million people)[d]	1996	448	154
	2007/2005	1071	137

Sources:

[a]Estimates from the Government of India–Ministry of Finance, Indian Economic Survey 2010–2011, http://indiabudget.nic.in/index.asp, accessed April 2011.
[b]World Economic Forum (2010).
[c]World Bank and International Finance Corporation (2010).
[d]World Bank, World Development Indicators, http://databank.worldbank.org, accessed April 2011.

Aubert (2001), China's challenge is how to adapt its economic strategy to embrace the knowledge and information revolution by developing appropriate institutions and providing incentives. The following are suggestions by Dahlman and Aubert (2001) for encouraging a shift into a knowledge- and services-based economy in China: (1) upgrading education and training linked to the needs of technology-intensive industries and services; (2) promoting greater use of information and communications technologies throughout the economy; (3) improving the dissemination and use of technology and related knowledge;

and (4) increasing public support for basic research, encouraging the manufacturing sector to do more research on its own, and promoting greater awareness of the importance of intellectual property rights.

Herstatt, Tiwari, Ernst, and Buse (2008) examine strengths and weaknesses in India's national innovation system based, in part, on information from interviews with firms, government, and institutions. They report that India is in the process of becoming a major R&D hub for multinationals in different industries due to the availability of cost-competitive technical manpower. They also find that firms are seeing benefits from R&D and planning to develop their R&D capacities. However, Herstatt et al. (2008) note that these positive developments are tempered by various impediments to national innovation system development, including technology infrastructure quality, overly bureaucratic rules, shortages of qualified and experienced manpower, and some institutions failing to reach international standards for cutting-edge R&D efforts. Not surprisingly, given the impediments in national innovation system development in India, R&D activity has tended to concentrate in large firms (Srinivasan and Archana, 2011). R&D is a risky activity with an uncertain outcome and large firms are better able to bear the costs of such activity as well as access low-cost project finance.

Investing in Infrastructure and Reducing Red Tape

Modern cost-competitive infrastructure (roads, railways, sea ports, power, and information technology) helps reduce trade costs, as well as provides a competitive advantage in exports and attracts inward investment. Similarly, an investment climate characterized by pro-business policies reduces business costs for enterprises engaged in foreign trade.

Enhancing cross-border infrastructure investment is a key area for intervention in the giants. ADB/ADB Institute (2009) identified a huge need for infrastructure investment in Asia, which was estimated to cost about $750 billion annually during 2010–2020. The study also identified about 20 priority infrastructure projects, including several involving the giants. With large financial reserves emanating from export surpluses, the giants can play an enhanced role in financing large multimodal, cross-border infrastructure projects involving neighboring economies and linking each other's markets. As table 13 shows, China (11 percent) spends more of its GDP on infrastructure than India (6 percent). China also fairs better than India on indicators of overall infrastructure quality, as well as the quality of roads and electricity supply, according to opinion surveys of businesspeople collected by the World Economic Forum.

Reducing bureaucratic impediments to conducting business is another key area. Table 13 provides information from the World Bank's "doing business" surveys on country ranks for the ease of starting a business, registering property, enforcing contracts, and closing a business. Also provided is an overall ease of doing business index that combines these indicators. Both giants scored relatively high on the World Bank's overall ease

> *The World Bank's 'ease of doing business' index places China higher than India*

of doing business index in 2010, meaning that they did less well compared with the world's top performers, but China seems better placed than India. China does better, in particular, in registering property, enforcing contracts, and closing a business.

Increasing Use of FTAs by Businesses

Section 5 suggested that the giants have pursued a variety of FTAs to liberalize the goods and services trade in the region, and that FTA use among Chinese firms was reasonable. Awareness of FTA provisions, however, varies among businesses in China and other Asian countries. Small- and medium-sized enterprises (SMEs) seem less well-informed than large firms and tend to use FTAs less often. Some firms also complain about cumbersome bureaucratic procedures associated with exporting through FTAs, such as stringent rules of origin and poor origin administration.

Accordingly, both giants (particularly India) need to adopt more proactive outreach measures to involve business associations in FTA negotiations and inform them of the benefits of FTAs through simple business guides and websites. They also need to adopt best practices in rules of origin in FTAs—coequality of rules, regional cumulation of origin, and origin administration by business associations—and enhance technical and other business support services to assist firms in making use of FTAs. In the medium term, a move toward a broad and deep Asia-wide FTA would significantly enhance business use of FTAs. It could provide a common and predictable policy framework for businesses, enable the realization of economies of scale, and lure inward investment (Chia 2010). Model-based studies suggest that an ASEAN+6 FTA—including China, India, Japan, South Korea, Australia, and New Zealand, along with the ASEAN economies, and covering goods, services, and trade facilitation—would bring higher welfare gains than alternative FTA scenarios. The formation of an ASEAN+6 FTA is expected to realize world income gains of around $260 billion (Kawai and Wignaraja 2011). There are active on-going discussions among Asian countries on the formation of such an Asia-wide FTA. In addition, the proposed expansion of the Transpacific Strategic Economic Partnership Agreement (or TPP) is attracting a growing number of Asian economies interested in its goal of a high-quality twenty-first century trade agreement. Over time, one may expect these two region-wide FTA processes to converge.

Managing Exchange Rates

China is now under international pressure to revalue its currency. Section 4 discussed China's exchange rate policy and export development. Recent policy attention, particularly in the United States, has been devoted to the links between the management of the renminbi, China's trade surplus, and the US trade deficit. It has been suggested that China's exchange rate does matter for global rebalancing. A recent econometric study by Cline (2010), for instance, estimates that at a 2010 scale, a 10 percent real effective appreciation would reduce China's current account surplus by $170 billion–$250 billion. The corresponding gain in the US current account balance would range from $22 billion–$63 billion. These findings have led to influential voices calling in early 2010 for stepped-up multilateral initiatives in the IMF and the WTO to promote appreciation of the exchange rate of the renminbi (Bergsten 2010).

China is now under international pressure to revalue its currency

On June 19, 2010, during the lead-up to the G-20 meeting in Toronto, the People's Bank of China announced that it would further reform the renminbi's exchange rate, thereby shifting to a more flexible exchange rate policy (Hu 2010). In particular, the announcement indicated continued emphasis on reflecting market supply and demand with reference to a currency basket, and maintaining wider exchange rate floating bands. Discussions in international fora and concerns about domestic inflation may lie behind the latest reforms. On September 29, 2010, the US House of Representatives passed legislation that would allow the United States to use estimates of currency undervaluation to calculate countervailing duties on imports from China and other countries. This move has sparked fears of a looming currency and trade war. A prolonged dispute over the currency issue could damage China-US trade and exert a negative impact on the two economies and the world economy. Accordingly, stepped-up international diplomacy to resolve the issue has been placed on the agenda of international fora such as the G-20 and exchange rates appear to be adjusting gradually. As India becomes more prominent in world export markets, it is possible that its exchange rate management may also emerge as an international policy issue.

Mitigating the Risk of Protectionism

High unemployment in the wake of the global financial crisis has prompted influential industrial lobby groups in G-20 economies to call for the protection of domestic industries. Mass public sector redundancies induced by government expenditure cuts are likely to accentuate such calls in the future. The available evidence suggests a modest rise in protectionist measures in G-20 economies since 2008, with emphasis on less transparent nontariff measures—particularly the sanitary and phytosanitary measures (SPS) and the technical barriers to trade (TBT)[13]—public procurement, and local buy-back schemes, rather than industrial tariffs per se.[14] There has also been a rise in antidumping and safeguard measures, with some targeting of highly competitive, labor-intensive exports from China and India. Concluding the WTO Doha Round offers the best insurance against rising protectionism, and a modest deal is better than no deal at all. The giants are well placed to steer WTO members toward a less ambitious Doha deal involving some reduction in agricultural subsidies and industrial tariffs, as well as trade facilitation. Such a deal may be supported by increased aid for trade and enhanced special and differential treatment to mitigate negative effects on lesser-developed and small, vulnerable economies. Whether this happens or not, China and India will influence the shape of the post-Doha trade agenda. In addition, China and India need to improve surveillance on nontariff measures in overseas markets, improve business support to cope with SPS and TBT measures affecting specific exports, and further upgrade legal capacity to deal with antidumping cases at the WTO.

Reducing Poverty

Section 2 suggested that reforms and swift trade expansions contributed to rising GDP per capita in the giants. The reforms were also expected to contribute to poverty reduction, as high levels of absolute poverty had characterized China and India for several decades. Table 14 provides comparable head-count poverty estimates at $1.25 per day (in purchasing power parity, or PPP) and $2 per day (in purchasing power parity), using household survey data from the World Bank. The most recent estimates for 2005 are somewhat dated, but still useful for illustrating the impact of economic reforms. At a poverty line of $1.25 per day, the share of the population in China that fell below the poverty line dropped from 84 percent to as low as 15.9 percent between 1981 and 2005. The same measure in India was 65.8 percent to 41.6 percent between 1978 and 2005. At a poverty line of $2 per day, the proportion of people below it dropped from 97.8 percent to 36.3 percent in China, and from 88.9 percent to 75.6 percent in India. China's achievement is unprecedented historically; it was able to take half a billion people out of poverty within 25 years. India also achieved poverty reduction, but not nearly as significantly.

Economic reforms and global integration did contribute to significant poverty reduction in China. Some decline in poverty occurred in the early reform period following the initial policy reforms. Between 1981 to 1990, the share of the population in poverty ($1.25 poverty line) fell from 84 percent to 60.2 percent. However, the greater fall in China occurred in the latter reform period, with poverty declining from 60.2 percent to 15.9 percent between 1990 and 2005. The expansion of labor-intensive

> *Poverty dropped sharply from 60.2 percent to 15.9 percent during China's latter reform period*

Table 14. Poverty Indicators, 1990 and 2005	CHINA	INDIA
Poverty at $1.25/day (PPP)		
No. of poor		
Earliest estimate[a]	803	463
1990	683	436
2005	208	456
Share of population (%)	81.5	20.0
Earliest estimate[a]	84.0	65.8
1990	60.2	51.3
2005	15.9	41.6
Poverty at $2.00/day (PPP)		
No. of poor	3.8	0.2
Earliest estimate[a]	972	625
1990/1988	961	683
2005	473	828
Share of population (%)	1.9	1.5
Earliest estimate[a]	97.8	88.9
1990/1988	84.6	83.8
2005	36.3	75.6
Memorandum items:		
	ASIA PACIFIC[b]	**WORLD**
Poverty at $1.25/day (PPP)		
No. of poor, 2005	903	1,400
% share of China and India	73.5	47.4
Poverty at $2.00/day (PPP)		
No. of poor, 2005	1,802	2,600
% share of China and India	72.2	50.0

Source: World Bank, World Development Indicators, http://databank.worldbank.org, accessed April 18, 2011.

Notes:

[a]Earliest estimate for India is 1978, and 1981 for China.

[b]Asia Pacific total only covers 25 countries where data are available.

manufactures provided employment and higher incomes, and it propelled millions out of poverty in China. There has been a steady decline in poverty in India since 1978, with little visible difference in the rate of poverty reduction between the immediate pre-reform periods (1978 and 1990) and post-reform periods (1990 and 2005). Bardhan (2010) suggests that the slower pace of poverty reduction in India than in China can be attributed to faster growth in China and greater elasticity of growth. In addition, he points to "differential inequalities of opportunity in the two countries" as another notable determinant (Bardhan 2010, 95). According to Bardhan, land ownership in much more unequal in India, India's poor have less access to education, and India is much more ethnically heterogeneous.

Furthermore, Sen (2011) suggests that some analysts have been obsessed with high growth in the giants as an end in itself while neglecting comparisons of the quality of life (e.g., life expectancy, education, and basic health) facilitated by growth. Sen suggests that current comparisons of the quality of life favor China over India. For instance, life expectancy at birth in China is 73.5 years but only 64.4 years in India. The mean years of schooling in China is 7.5 years; in India it is 4.4 years. The infant mortality rate is 17 per thousand in China compared with 50 in India.

When more recent post-2005 data on absolute poverty is available, further analysis would be invaluable on the links between economic reforms, exports, and poverty reduction in the giants. Recent issues of particular interest would include the impact on poverty of the global financial crisis and rising food prices. While a historic decline has been achieved particularly in China, poverty reduction remains an important goal for future trade-led growth in the giants. The magnitude of poverty in the giants is striking. The latest comparable estimates suggest that, in 2005, as many as 664 million in both countries still fell below a poverty line of $1.25 a day. Sustaining rapid economic growth, promoting labor-intensive manufactured exports, and increasing social expenditures (on health, education, and nutrition) are all important poverty reduction strategies in the giants.

7. Conclusions

The switch to market-oriented economic reforms in China and India represents a turning point in the history of economic development. At the time, however, few foresaw the future impact the giants would collectively have on world trade patterns or the magnitude of adjustment required in the rest of the world. The growing body of research analyzing the link between trade performance and economic reforms seems to have drawn mixed conclusions on causality. Accordingly, against the backdrop of recovery from the global financial crisis, this paper attempted a re-appraisal of the links between economic reforms and exports in China and India. Four questions were analyzed: (1) Have China's exports outpaced India's since the reforms? (2) What roles have initial conditions, as well as liberalization of trade and investment regimes, played in the giants' export records? (3) Is the giants' recent emphasis on FTAs detrimental to exports? (4) What are the emerging policy challenges in the post–global financial crisis era?

The main findings from the paper are as follows.

First, the trade performance of China and India has been impressive by historical standards. Within a relatively short time span of about a generation, the giants have emerged as major players in world trade, as well as notable outward investors. Following early entry into low-technology products, the giants have steadily upgraded into medium- and high-technology products, as well as skill-intensive services.

China is on the verge of challenging the United States as the world's largest exporter

While the two are often compared, China has roared ahead in world trade in manufactures and is on the verge of challenging the United States as the world's largest exporter. India's export expansion has been primarily driven by services, and it is attempting to play catch-up in a range of manufactured exports.

Second, a combination of initial conditions and changes in policies underlie export success in the giants. The outcome of economic reforms on trade performance was shaped by initial conditions. These include China's proximity to Japan, which facilitated inward investment and a large, dynamic domestic market. Township and village enterprises (TVEs) also seem to have initially led labor-intensive rural industrialization in China. Both India and China had access to ample supplies of low-cost, productive manpower. India's relative success in information technology and business process outsourcing seems linked to exposure to English, world-class IT professionals and engineers, and close links with an IT-oriented diaspora.

The reforms, particularly those of trade and investment, have played a significant role in the trade performance of China and India. China, of course, was swifter and introduced an open door policy toward export-oriented FDI in the late 1970s, alongside controlled liberalization of imports. Further liberalization occurred in China during the process of WTO accession. India introduced some reforms in the late 1970s, but the major reforms came after 1991. The difference in trade performance between China and India, however, is not simply a matter of the timing of changes in trade and investment policies. Closer examination suggests China adopted a more comprehensive and pro-active approach to trade and industrial

> *India's 1991 economic reforms marked the end of the license raj*

policy than India. Differences were apparent in China's approach in attracting export-oriented FDI, actively facilitating technological upgrading of FDI and exports, reducing import tariffs and their dispersion in a more systematic manner, managing a more predictable and transparent real exchange rate, and providing for more comprehensive liberalization in goods and services provisions in its FTAs with Asian developing economies.

Third, China's and India's FTAs do not seem to be having a detrimental effect on exports. The giants' FTA strategies still appear to be in the formative stages. China's FTAs with regional developing economies are geared towards supporting its role as the global factory and the deepening of its production networks. From an initial focus on South-South trade, India has recently moved towards seeking market access to East Asia and major developed countries. China's FTAs seem to have better coverage in terms of goods and services. FTA use at least in China also seems higher than expected. Nonetheless, both countries can improve the coverage of Singapore issues in future FTAs and adopt best practices in designing rules of origin and origin administration.

Fourth, following a decade of tentative reform, India accelerated its reform agenda to match China and other industrial leaders. In particular, India adopted appropriate trade and investment policies, particularly on attracting export-oriented FDI and liberalizing tariffs. It is also entering into ambitious FTA negotiations with developed countries, which could provide market access and FDI inflows, among other benefits. Therefore, one might reasonably expect the gap in trade and investment performance between the giants to narrow over time, but with China's dominance in manufactures to continue for at least the next decade.[15]

Some popular accounts (e.g., see the *Economist*, October 2, 2010) predict that India's growth may overtake China's by 2013. Several factors are

> ### *Some predict that India's growth may overtake China's by 2013*

said to be in India's favor, including a relatively young and growing workforce, a base of world-class companies led by English-speaking bosses, and democratic institutions. Weighed against this is a much larger export base than in China; much higher levels of investment in R&D, skills, and infrastructure; and better policy coordination and implementation.

Fifth, both China and India face a new and more uncertain world economic environment in the post–global financial crisis era. The global financial crisis has marked the end a period of respectable world growth and expanding employment in major industrial economies. The likely scenario for the medium term seems to be slow growth and high unemployment in large swaths of the developed world. China and India have seen rebounding growth since the global financial crisis, and they have contributed to world growth during and after the crisis. However, it is unclear how much longer the giants can extend this role without a stronger recovery in the developed world. Without strong demand from developed markets, the two giants will increasingly have to rely on inter-Asian demand and South-South cooperation for continued growth and exports.

Finally, myriad policy challenges are likely to impinge on the pace of trade-led growth in the giants in the new macroeconomic era. Challenges include entering production networks, promoting industrial technology development, investing in infrastructure and reducing red tape, increasing FTA use by businesses, managing exchange rates, mitigating the risk of protectionism, and reducing poverty. The giants' trade performance will depend largely on how each copes with these challenges. A coherent strategy that blends economic reform with regional cooperation can result in a virtuous cycle of sustained export growth and rising income as the seeds for future global prosperity.

Endnotes

1. The literature on economic reforms and trade in the giants is vast, and an exhaustive survey is beyond the scope of this paper. On China, see the pioneering studies by Lardy (2002), Huang (2008), Zhang (2009), and the collection of papers in Feenstra and Wei (2010). On India, see Panagariya (2004), Kumar and Sharma (2009), and Bardhan (2010). Useful comparative economic studies include: Amsden (2001), Winters and Yusuf (2007), Panagariya (2007), Anantaram and Saqib (2010), and Kowalski (2010).

2. In 2010, China's merchandise exports ($1.58 trillion) were larger than those of the US ($1.28 trillion). But the US ($515 billion) is a larger service exporter than China ($170 billion). See WTO (2011).

3. The 1995 and 2005 figures are from Anantaram and Saqib (2010, 141), while the 2010 (January to August) data are from www.fdi.gov.cn.

4. Zhang et al. (1998) evaluate the structure of trade protection in China and present estimates of static costs. They suggest that trade liberalization would lead to short-term costs in terms of lost domestic output and employment, but estimate long-run benefits to be in the range of about $35 billion.

5. Lall's pioneering study of the acquisition of technological capabilities in Indian industry during the early 1980s concludes, "Even the leading enterprises find themselves unable to undertake the development of major new products and process technologies. More interestingly, they find it difficult to copy many new advances in product technology (for sophisticated new equipment, for instance) on their own." (Lall 1987, 238).

6. See Kawai and Wignaraja (2011).

7. These are Norway, Switzerland, Iceland, and Liechtenstein.

8. Trade facilitation refers to the simplification and harmonization of the customs procedures that regulate international trade, with the intent of reducing cost burdens while safeguarding legitimate regulatory objectives.

9. I am grateful to Richard Baldwin for this point.

10. Meetings with FICCI officials, including Manab Majumdar (Assistant Secretary-General, FICCI) and Manish Mohan (Senior Director, FICCI), in New Delhi, April 12, 2010. For an early assessment of the Indo-Lanka FTA and lessons of the experience, see Kelegama and Mukherji (2007).

11. I am grateful to Garry Hufbauer for a discussion on medium-term world growth prospects.

12. According to Feenstra and Wei (2010), ordinary trade includes imports that enter the country and that are not destined to be incorporated into exported goods (or exports that did not rely specifically on imported inputs). Meanwhile, processing trade includes imports that enter the country duty-free and that will be incorporated into exported goods, as well as exports that rely on these processing imports.

13. During the Uruguay Round of multilateral trade negotiations, member nations established the Agreement on the Application of Sanitary and Phytosanitary Measures (SPS Agreement) and the Agreement on Technical Barriers to Trade (TBT Agreement) to address the emerging debate over the use of standards in international trade. Generally speaking, the SPS Agreement is a compromise that permits countries to take measures to protect public health within their borders, as long as they do so in a manner that restricts trade as little as possible. Similarly, the TBT Agreement strikes a delicate balance between the policy goals of trade facilitation and national autonomy in technical regulations.

14. OECD, WTO, and UNCTAD (2010) suggests that new import-restricting measures introduced on September 1, 2009, covered 0.7% of G-20 imports and 0.4% of total world imports through mid-February 2010. Similar figures for October 2008–October 2009 were 1.3% and 0.8%, respectively. The joint report concludes that there was no indication of a significant increase of trade or investment restriction during the period under review, but notes that some G-20 members have continued to put in place measures that potentially restrict trade, directly or indirectly. New trade restrictions tend to be concentrated in sectors that are relatively protected and also relatively labor-intensive, including minerals, textiles, and metal products.

15. I am grateful to Alan Winters for clarifying this point about the giants' future prospects.

Bibliography

Asian Development Bank. 2011a. *Asian Development Outlook 2011*. Manila: Asian Development Bank.

Asian Develoment Bank. 2011b. *Institutions for Regional Integration: Toward an Asian Economic Community*. Manila: Asian Development Bank.

Asian Development Bank and Asian Development Bank Institute. 2009. *Infrastructure for a Seamless Asia*. Manila: Asian Development Bank / Tokyo: Asian Development Bank Institute.

Amsden, A. 2001. *The Rise of "the Rest": Challenges to the West from Late-Industrializing Economies*. Oxford, UK: Oxford University Press.

Anantaram, R., and M. Saqib. 2010. "The People's Republic of China's Manufacturing Sector Since 1978." In Gerhaeusser, K., Y. Iwasaki, and V.B. Tulasidhar, eds. *Resurging Asian Giants: Lessons from the People's Republic of China and India*. Manila: Asian Development Bank.

Athukorala, P. 2009. "Outward Foreign Direct Investment from India." *Asian Development Review* 26(2): 125–153.

Balassa, B. 1977. A Stages Approach to Comparative Advantage," World Bank Staff Working Paper, no. 256, (World Bank, Washington, DC).

Baldwin, R.E. 2008. "Managing the Noodle Bowl: The Fragility of East Asian Regionalism." *The Singapore Economic Review* 53(3): 449–478.

Bardhan, P. 2010. *Awakening the Giants: Feet of Clay*. Princeton, NJ: Princeton University Press.

Batra, A., and Z. Khan. 2005. "Revealed Comparative Advantage: An Analysis for India and China," ICRIER Working Paper, no. 168 (Indian Council for Research on International Economic Relations, New Delhi).

Bergsten, F.C. 2010. "Correcting the Chinese Exchange Rate: An Action Plan," Testimony before the Committee on Ways and Means, US House of Representatives, March 24, 2010. Available at the Petersen Institute for International Economics, Washington, DC, www.piie.com.

Bhagwati, J.N., and P. Desai. 1970. *India: Planning for Industrialization.* Oxford, UK: Oxford University Press.

Borrus, M., D. Ernst, and S. Haggard, eds. 2000. *International Production Networks in Asia: Rivalry or Riches.* London: Routledge.

Bowen, C. 2010. "China's WTO Entry: Antidumping, Safeguards and Dispute Settlement." In Feenstra, R.C., and S.J. Wei, eds. 2010. *China's Growing Role in World Trade.* Chicago: Chicago University Press.

Chia, S.Y. 2010. "Regional Trade Policy Cooperation and Architecture in East Asia," ADBI Working Paper Series, no. 191 (Asian Development Bank Institute, Tokyo, February).

Cline, W. 2010. "Renminbi Undervaluation, China's Surplus, and the US Trade Deficit," *Peterson Institute for International Economics Policy Brief No. PB10–20,* August.

Dahlman, C.J., and J. Aubert. 2001. *China and the Knowledge Economy: Seizing the 21st Century.* WBI Development Studies. Washington, DC: The World Bank Institute.

Davies, K. 2010. "Outward FDI from China and Its Policy Content," In *Columbia FDI Profiles,* Vale Columbia Center on Sustainable Development, New York, October 18.

Economist (2010), "How India's Growth Will Outpace China's," October 2, print edition.

Feenstra, R.C., and S.J. Wei. 2010. "Introduction." In Feenstra, R.C., and S.J. Wei, eds. 2010. *China's Growing Role in World Trade.* Chicago: Chicago University Press.

Gerhaeusser, K., Y. Iwasaki, and V.B. Tulasidhar, eds. 2010. *Resurging Asian Giants: Lessons from the People's Republic of China and India.* Manila: Asian Development Bank.

Government of India–Ministry of Commerce and Industry. 2011. "Fact Sheet on Foreign Direct Investment (August 1991 to December 2010)," http://dipp.nic.in/fdi_statistics/india_FDI_December2010.pdf, accessed April 2011.

Government of India–Ministry of Finance. 2010. "Indian Economic Survey 2010–2011," http://indiabudget.nic.in/index.asp, accessed April 2011.

Government of the People's Republic of China–Ministry of Commerce. 2011. "Statistics of China's Absorption of FDI from January to December 2010," http://english.mofcom.gov.cn/aarticle/statistic/foreigninvestment/201101/20110107381641.html, accessed April 2011.

Herstatt, C., R. Tiwari, D. Ernst, and S. Buse. 2008. "India's National Innovation System: Key Elements and Corporate Perspectives," East-West Center Working Papers, Economic Series, no. 96 (East-West Center, Honolulu, August).

Holscher, J., E. Marelli, and M. Signorelli. 2010. "China and India in the Global Economy." *Economic Systems* 34: 212–217.

Hu, X. 2010. "A Managed Floating Exchange Rate Regime is an Established Policy." Speech at the People's Bank of China, July 15, Beijing, available at www.pbc .gov.cn. Accessed April 2011.

Huang, Y. 2008. *Capitalism with Chinese Characteristics.* New York City: Cambridge University Press.

Kawai, M., and G. Wignaraja. 2011. "Asian FTAs: Trends, Challenges and Prospects." *Journal of Asian Economics* 22: 1–22.

———, eds. 2011. *Asia's Free Trade Agreements: How Is Business Responding?* Cheltenham, UK: Edward Elgar.

Kelegama, S., and I.N. Mukherji. 2007. "India-Sri Lanka Bilateral Free Trade Agreement: Six Years Performance and Beyond," RIS Discussion Papers. no. 119 (Research and Information System for Developing Countries, New Delhi).

Kowalski, P. 2010. "China and India: A Tale of Two Trade Integration Approaches." In Eichengreen, B., P. Gupta, and R. Kumar, eds. 2010. *Emerging Giants: China and India in the World Economy.* Oxford, UK: Oxford University Press.

Kumar, N., and P. Sharma. 2009. "India." In Francois, J., P. Rana, and G. Wignaraja, eds. 2009. *National Strategies for Regional Integration: South and East Asian Case Studies.* London: Anthem Press.

Lall, S. 1987. *Learning to Industrialize: The Acquisition of Technological Capability by India.* Basingstoke, UK: Macmillan Press.

———. 2001. *Competitiveness, Technology and Skills.* Cheltenham, UK: Edward Elgar.

Lardy, N.R. 2002. *Integrating China into the Global Economy.* Washington, DC: Brooking Institution Press.

———. 2003. "Trade Liberalization and Its Role in Chinese Economic Growth." Paper prepared for an IMF and NCAER conference, "A Tale of Two Giants: India's and China's Experience with Reform and Growth," New Delhi, November 14–16, 2003.

Maddison, A. 2007. *Chinese Economic Performance in the Long Run: 960–2030 AD.* Paris: OECD Publishing.

Mathews, J.A., and D.S. Cho. 2000. *Tiger Technology: The Creation of a Semi-Conductor Industry in East Asia.* Cambridge, UK: Cambridge University Press.

OECD (Organisation for Economic Co-operation and Development), WTO (World Trade Organization), and UNCTAD (United Nations Conference on Trade and Development). 2010. *Report on G20 Trade and Investment Measures, September 2009 to February 2010.* Paris and Geneva: OECD, WTO, and UNCTAD.

Panagariya, A. 2004. "India's Trade Reform." In Berry, S., B. Bosworth, and A. Panagariya, eds. *India Policy Forum 2004*, vol. 1. New Delhi: National Council of Applied Economic Research / Washington, DC: Brookings Institution Press.

———. 2006. "India and China: Trade and Foreign Investment," Stanford Center for International Development Working Paper, no. 302 (Stanford University, Stanford, CA, November).

————. 2007. "Why India Lags Behind China and How It Can Bridge the Gap." *World Economy* 30(2): 229–248.

Petri, P. 2008. *Multitrack Integration in East Asian Trade: Noodle Bowl or Matrix?* Asia-Pacific Issues, no. 86 (Honolulu: East-West Center, October).

Plummer, M. 2007. "Best Practices in Regional Trade Agreements: An Application to Asia." *World Economy* 30(12): 1771–1796.

Rodrick, D. 2006. "What's So Special About China's Exports?" NBER Working Paper, no. 11947 (National Bureau of Economic Research, Cambridge, MA).

Sen, A.K. 2011. "Quality of Life: China vs. India", The New York Review of Books, May 12, 58:8. www.nybooks.com. Accessed June 2011.

Srinivasan, T.N. and V. Archana. 2011. "Determinants of Export Decision of Firms." *Economic and Political Weekly*, 46(7): 49-58.

Suominen, K. 2009. "The Changing Anatomy of Regional Trade Agreements in East Asia." *Journal of East Asian Studies* 9(1): 29–56.

Wignaraja, G. 2003. "Competitiveness Analysis and Strategy." In Wignaraja, G., ed. 2003. *Competitiveness Strategy in Developing Countries.* London: Routledge.

————. 2008. "Ownership, Technology and Buyers: Explaining Exporting in China and Sri Lanka." *Transnational Corporations* 17(2): 1–15.

————. 2010. "Are ASEAN FTAs Used for Exporting?" In Gugler, P., and J. Chaisee, eds. 2010. *Competitiveness of the ASEAN Countries: Corporate and Regulatory Drivers.* Cheltenham, UK: Edward Elgar.

————. 2011. "Innovation, Learning and Exporting in China: Does R&D or a Technology Index Matter?" *Journal of Asian Economics*, doi:10.1016/j.asieco .2011.02.001 (article in press).

Wignaraja, G., and D. Lazaro. 2010. "North-South vs. South-South Asian FTAs: Trends, Compatibilities, and Ways Forward," UNU-CRIS Working Papers, no. W-2010/3 (United Nations University Institute on Comparative Regional Integration Studies, Bruges, Belgium).

Winters, A., and S. Yusuf. 2007. "Introduction." In Winters, A. and S. Yusuf, eds. 2007. *Dancing with the Giants: China, India and the Global Economy.* Washington, DC: World Bank Publications.

World Bank. 2011. World Development Indicators, http://databank.worldbank.org.

World Bank and International Finance Corporation. 2010. *Doing Business 2011: Making a Difference for Entrepreneurs.* Washington, DC: World Bank Publications.

World Economic Forum. 2010. *The Global Competitiveness Report 2010–11.* Geneva: World Economic Forum.

World Trade Organization. 2007. *Trade Policy Review: India.* Geneva: World Trade Organization.

————. 2010. *Trade Policy Review: China.* Geneva: World Trade Organization.

———. 2011. "World Trade 2010, Prospects for 2011: Trade Growth to Ease in 2011 But Despite 2010 Record Surge, Crisis Hangover Persists," press release, available at http://www.wto.org/english/news_e/pres11_e/pr628_e.htm. Accessed April 2011

Yusuf, S., K. Nabeshima, and D.H. Perkins. 2007. "China and India Reshape Global Industrial Geography." In Winters, A. and S. Yusuf, eds. 2007. *Dancing with the Giants: China, India and the Global Economy.* Washington, DC: World Bank Publications.

Zhang, Y. 2009. "People's Republic of China." In Francois, J., P. Rana, and G. Wignaraja, eds. 2009. *National Strategies for Regional Integration: South and East Asian Case Studies.* London: Anthem Press.

———. 2011. "People's Republic of China." In Kawai, M., and G. Wignaraja, eds. 2011. *Asia's Free Trade Agreements: How Is Business Responding?* Cheltenham, UK: Edward Elgar.

Zhang, Y., W. Zhongxin, and S. Zhang. 1998. *Measuring the Costs of Protection in China.* Washington, DC: Peterson Institute for International Economics.

Acknowledgments

The views expressed here are solely the author's and should not be attributed to the Asian Development Bank. I am most grateful to Dieter Ernst, Lei Lei Song, Max Kreinin, Michael Plummer, and two referees for comments; to Anna-Mae Tuazon for research assistance; and Elisa Johnston for publication support.

Policy Studies series

A publication of the East-West Center

Series Editors: Edward Aspinall and Dieter Ernst

Description
Policy Studies provides policy-relevant scholarly analysis of key contemporary domestic and international issues affecting Asia. The editors invite contributions on Asia's economics, politics, security, and international relations.

Notes to Contributors
Submissions may take the form of a proposal or complete manuscript. For more information on the Policy Studies series, please contact the Series Editors.

Editors, *Policy Studies*
East-West Center
1601 East-West Road
Honolulu, Hawai'i 96848-1601
Tel: 808.944.7197
Publications@EastWestCenter.org
EastWestCenter.org/policystudies

www.ingramcontent.com/pod-product-compliance
Lightning Source LLC
Chambersburg PA
CBHW050547280326
41933CB00011B/1759